Managing Born-Digital Special Collections and Archival Materials

SPEC Kits

Supporting Effective Library Management for Nearly 40 Years

Committed to assisting research and academic libraries in the continuous improvement of management systems, ARL has worked since 1970 to gather and disseminate the best practices for library needs. As part of its commitment, ARL maintains an active publications program best known for its SPEC Kits. Through the Collaborative Research/Writing Program, librarians work with ARL staff to design SPEC surveys and write publications. Originally established as an information source for ARL member libraries, the SPEC Kit series has grown to serve the needs of the library community worldwide.

What are SPEC Kits?

Published six times per year, SPEC Kits contain the most valuable, up-to-date information on the latest issues of concern to libraries and librarians today. They are the result of a systematic survey of ARL member libraries on a particular topic related to current practice in the field. Each SPEC Kit contains an executive summary of the survey results; survey questions with tallies and selected comments; the best representative documents from survey participants, such as policies, procedures, handbooks, guidelines, Web sites, records, brochures, and statements; and a selected reading list—both print and online sources—containing the most current literature available on the topic for further study.

Subscribe to SPEC Kits

Subscribers tell us that the information contained in SPEC Kits is valuable to a variety of users, both inside and outside the library. SPEC Kit purchasers use the documentation found in SPEC Kits as a point of departure for research and problem solving because they lend immediate authority to proposals and set standards for designing programs or writing procedure statements. SPEC Kits also function as an important reference tool for library administrators, staff, students, and professionals in allied disciplines who may not have access to this kind of information.

SPEC Kits are available in print and online. For more information visit: **http://www.arl.org/resources/pubs/**. The executive summary for each kit after December 1993 can be accessed free of charge at **http://www.arl.org/resources/pubs/spec/complete.shtml**.

SPEC Kit 329

Managing Born-Digital Special Collections and
Archival Materials

August 2012

Naomi L. Nelson and Seth Shaw

Duke University

Nancy Deromedi and Michael Shallcross

University of Michigan

Cynthia Ghering and Lisa Schmidt

Michigan State University

Michelle Belden, Jackie R. Esposito, Ben Goldman, and Tim Pyatt

Pennsylvania State University

ASSOCIATION OF RESEARCH LIBRARIES

Series Editor: Lee Anne George

SPEC Kits are published by the

Association of Research Libraries
21 Dupont Circle, NW, Suite 800
Washington, DC 20036-1118
P (202) 296-2296 F (202) 872-0884
http://www.arl.org/resources/pubs/spec/
pubs@arl.org

ISSN 0160 3582

ISBN 1-59407-883-1 / 978-1-59407-883-5 print
ISBN 1-59407-884-X / 978-1-59407-884-2 online

Copyright © 2012

SPEC
Kit 329

Managing Born-Digital Special Collections and
Archival Materials

August 2012

SURVEY RESULTS

REPRESENTATIVE DOCUMENTS

SELECTED RESOURCES

SURVEY RESULTS

EXECUTIVE SUMMARY

Introduction

The 2010 OCLC Research report, *Taking Our Pulse*, listed management of born-digital materials as the third biggest challenge facing libraries, special collections, and archives, after space and facilities. It has become a truism that the trickle of born-digital materials into special collections has become a flood. Increasingly, these materials do not have analog counterparts. Libraries and archives can no longer defer decisions about digital content to a later date. We must develop policies and procedures to operationalize the management of born-digital materials, or we risk losing the record of the recent past.

This survey sought to gather and promote emerging good practices for managing born-digital content and to highlight common challenges. The survey instrument focused in particular on staffing, ingest and processing workflows, storage procedures, and access and discovery methods. Sixty-four of the 126 ARL member libraries responded to the survey between February 22 and March 23 for a response rate of 51%. Fifty-nine of the respondents (92%) already collect born-digital content. The remaining five libraries are in the planning stages. The level of engagement with born-digital content was higher than anticipated by the survey team. An analysis of the responding libraries engaged with born-digital materials revealed they are larger institutions and therefore more likely to be pioneers in working with this content.

The management of born-digital materials is still relatively new for ARL libraries, and the survey results show that good practices and workflows are still evolving. New tools are emerging rapidly, and the once-solid line between digitized content and born-digital content is beginning to blur. Survey responses indicated that the library and archives profession lacks a common definition of what born-digital content is and a common understanding of who within the organization should manage this content.

Staffing and Organization

The survey asked how many library staff collect and manage born-digital materials, who has responsibility for storage-related activities, how staffing needs are addressed, and how staff gain the expertise required to manage these materials. No one staffing or organizational structure emerged from the survey responses, which again reflects the evolutionary status of born-digital management programs.

The number of staff working with born-digital archival content in the responding libraries ranges from less than one to 60 FTE. While archivists and librarians in institutional and government archives were the trailblazers in collecting this content, managing these materials now requires staff from digitization, digital curation, information technology, and institutional repository units. Respondents most frequently mentioned special collections/archives staff and library IT staff as having decision-making responsibility for selecting storage solutions, implementing and maintaining infrastructure, managing user authentication, estimating storage needs and monitoring usage, and budgeting. Many other units are also involved, including institutional IT, preservation, collections, administration, and consortia in a wide variety of combinations.

This organizational distribution may factor into how respondents have addressed staffing needs for managing born-digital content. Almost all have used a combination of strategies, either adding that responsibility to existing positions (94%) or recasting an existing position (37%), and creating new positions (46%). Training strategies reflect the emphasis on retooling the skill sets of existing positions. Conferences, on-the-job training, workshops, and independent study are the primary methods staff use to develop their expertise with born-digital content.

Born-Digital Materials Collected

Almost all of the responding libraries (54 or 84%) are currently collecting electronic theses and dissertations. The majority also collect personal archives and institutional records and archives. Most of the others report they plan to collect these categories of materials. Twenty-one libraries collect research data and 28 others plan to collect it. Photographs, audio and video recordings, texts, and moving images are the most frequently collected media formats. About a third of the respondents collect websites, email, and databases; almost an equal number plan to collect these formats. While only six currently collect social media, 23 others plan to do so in the future.

Ingest Policies and Procedures

The majority of respondents (45 or 71%) have not developed gift/purchase agreement language that is specific to born-digital materials, but many are reviewing those agreements. Thirty-six respondents (56%) reported that they have developed ingest and processing workflows. An analysis of the comments indicates that a number of libraries are in the development phase. The comments also revealed a variety of models and/or examples the libraries have used in the development of workflows. These influences can be grouped into nine general categories as seen in the chart below.

Projects that influenced workflow development include the Personal Archives Accessible in Digital Media (PARADIGM) and futureArch projects at the University of Oxford's Bodleian Library, the AIMS project (Born Digital Collections: An Inter-Institutional Model for Stewardship) conducted by Stanford University, Yale University, University of Virginia, and University of Hull (UK), InterPARES, the British Library's Digital Lives project, the Tufts Accessioning Program for Electronic Records (TAPER) project, the European Union's Preservation

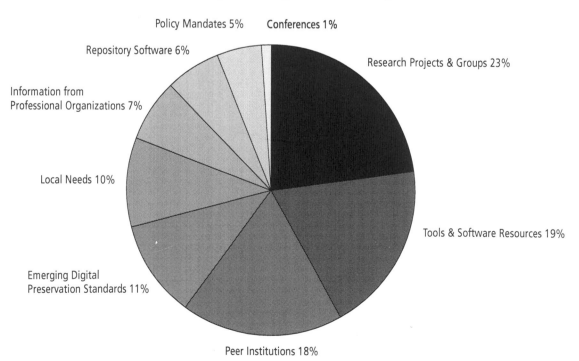

Influences on the Development of Ingest and Processing Workflows

Policy Mandates 5% Conferences 1%
Repository Software 6%
Information from Professional Organizations 7%
Research Projects & Groups 23%
Local Needs 10%
Tools & Software Resources 19%
Emerging Digital Preservation Standards 11%
Peer Institutions 18%

and Long-term Access through Networked Services (PLANETS) project, and the Sustainable Archives & Leveraging Technologies (SALT) research group at the University of North Carolina.

Influential tools and software resources include Archivematica, the Duke Data Accessioner, digital forensics tools (including AccessData FTK Imager), file identification and validation tools (such as DROID and JHOVE), and the University of North Carolina's Curator's Workbench.

Respondents highlighted documentation made available by the Interuniversity Consortium for Political and Social Research (ICPSR) at the University of Michigan, the Digital Preservation Management workshop developed at Cornell University, the University of Illinois's IDEALS (Illinois Digital Environment for Access to Learning and Scholarship) repository, the California Digital Library's Merritt repository, Stanford's digital forensics lab, Emory University's Salman Rushdie collection, and Chris Prom's Practical E-Records blog.

Standards that influenced workflow development include the Open Archival Information System (OAIS) Reference Model, the PREMIS (PREservation Metadata: Implementation Strategies) metadata schema, the SWORD (Simple Web-service Offering Repository Deposit) protocol, and the BagIt specification.

Information provided by the MetaArchive, the National Digital Information Infrastructure and Preservation Program (NDIIPP), and professional journals, as well as the Digital Curation Centre's life-cycle model, influenced several respondents.

Perhaps as a sign of how workflows are tailored to fit local resources, some respondents cited DSpace repository software and CONTENTdm as influences on workflows. A few cited policy guidelines and mandates from parent organizations. Others mentioned Society of American Archivists and Midwest Archives Conference panel presentations on practical approaches to born-digital records, although no one mentioned conferences such as iPRES or the Personal Digital Archiving conference for which born-digital content is the specific focus.

While it appears that many respondents do not yet have well-established workflows for the ingest and processing of digital content, the majority are actively addressing the challenges of preparing born-digital content for long-term preservation and access.

Ingest Strategies

Seventy-seven percent of the responding libraries are ingesting born-digital records that are stored on legacy media. Almost all of them are storing the media "as is," and about half are collecting hardware that can retrieve data from those media. Fifteen libraries (25%) are outsourcing data retrieval and another 20 (33%) are planning to use that strategy. Only eight libraries are building new systems that replicate the function of the legacy systems. Other strategies include migrating content from legacy media to a storage location (described variously as "server storage" or "dark archives" space) and converting legacy born-digital content to "modern," "less proprietary," or "the latest usable" formats that include CSV files and PDF/A files.

Storage Solutions

The survey asked which kinds of storage media are used for ingest, processing, access, back up, and long-term dark storage functions. Most respondents use a combination of external media, network file systems, and local storage for all functions. Only 12 respondents (19%) report using cloud storage.

Local/attached storage (46 responses or 75%) and external media library (41 or 67%) were the most prevalent ingest solutions, followed closely by a network file system (35 or 57%). Other solutions include the DSpace-based commercial hosted Open Repository, the OnBase commercial enterprise content management system, and an institution's collection development instance of DSpace. One respondent stated that they are currently using cloud storage on a limited basis for ingest, and "plan to investigate its use for the other categories." Another belongs to a consortium that provides web-based ingest, processing, and access for ETDs, presumably including storage.

The most prevalent processing storage solutions are a network file system and local/attached storage, both at 43 responses (75%). External media library was a distant third. Other solutions were the same as for ingest: the consortium, the collection development instance of DSpace, and OnBase.

The most used access storage solution is a network file system (43 responses or 72%). External media library and local/attached storage each received 27 responses (45%). One respondent noted that they use Amazon Cloud and hosted Open Repository. Another uses a local DSpace instance, the California Digital Library's web archiving service, and a university system-wide open access repository. Other solutions include the use of a local implementation of a Fedora repository, YouSendIt online file sharing software in combination with e-mail, and shared IT servers.

The most common back up storage solution is a network file system (44 responses or 76%), followed by external media library (31 or 53%), local/attached storage (23 or 40%), and distributed systems (16 or 28%). Other solutions include a combination of Amazon Cloud and hosted Open Repository, the California Digital Library's Merritt Repository, redundant storage managed by campus and library IT, and physical tape storage.

Network file systems are used most for dark storage (26 responses or 52%), with distributed computing/storage systems second (19 or 38%). External media library and local/attached storage were not far behind at 16 and 14 responses, respectively. Other dark storage solutions include the California Digital Library's Merritt Repository, the Chronopolis digital preservation network, the Isilon commercial storage platform, redundant storage managed by campus and library IT, and virtual and physical tape storage. One respondent stated that rather than dark storage, their institution uses Fedora as an asset management system and copies files to "replicated storage for long-term preservation, with appropriate preservation metadata and restricted access."

Estimating Storage Needs and Costs

Twenty-six of the responding libraries (59%) estimate future digital storage needs and costs based on past and current usage and/or planned growth. Three noted that storage is allocated on a case-by-case basis. Some respondents have yet to implement methods of estimating storage needs and costs. Others are in the process of developing such methods.

Respondents described a variety of approaches to estimating storage needs and costs. One is conducting a longitudinal analysis of trends in digital storage growth. Another will scale future digital storage needs to the "development of campus department operations." Another currently uses costs of disks, storage devices, and backups as the basis for total cost estimates and is looking at moving to endowment-based storage cost models in the future. One respondent anticipates using the L.I.F.E. (Life Cycle Information for E-Literature) model developed by University College London (UCL) and the British Library for estimating curation costs, including the cost of storage.

One institution estimates space needs based on "past collecting volume + a 20% inflator + any known collections we anticipate receiving." Another estimates required storage needs based on average file size for a particular type of record and then estimates costs based on the current market value of storage, "usually at the TB level."

The most detailed response described the institution's attempt to estimate storage needs by tracking historical usage and growth, contrasting those with earlier projections, and categorizing data by type to identify growth areas. Thus far, the respondent observes that "consumption generally increases by a factor of 2 to 4 within a 12–18 month period," but any projection can change when unexpected projects or changes in the organization occur.

Access and Discovery

The survey asked which delivery methods the library uses to provide access to born-digital materials. Two-thirds of respondents provide online access to a digital repository system. Just under half provide in-library access on a dedicated workstation. Users who bring their PCs to 22 of the responding libraries can access born-digital materials stored on portable media. Eighteen respondents (28%) use third-party systems such as CONTENTdm, Archive-It, Dropbox, and YouTube to share materials with researchers.

There is not one, single repository system being used either to manage or provide access to born-digital materials. Most respondents use open source repository software for both management and access functions. Twenty-eight institutions report using secure file system storage to manage collections but only ten use it to provide access. The results seem to suggest that access to collections is not as fully developed as the management of born-digital content.

The survey asked whether the institution is using different types of repositories for different types of born-digital materials. While 63% reported that they are, their comments indicate that they use different repositories for a variety of reasons, including media type (e.g., images, audio/visual materials, websites), record type (e.g., thesis and dissertations, faculty preprints), access and preservation requirements, and whether the material is digitized or born digital.

Ingest Challenges

The challenges related to the ingest of born-digital materials can be grouped into three broad categories: the difficulties associated with accessing information stored on legacy media and/or in obsolete file formats; the lack of policies, end-to-end workflows, and robust, integrated systems for digital object ingest; and the need to scale up to meet the increasing volume of born-digital objects needing preservation.

The challenges related to working with legacy formats and hardware were the most frequently cited ingest issues (43% of respondents listed file format or software obsolescence; 38% included legacy media or hardware). Donors, campus offices, and other records creators place their materials in a library or archives when they are no longer actively using them. As a result, libraries often receive storage media (punch cards, floppy disks, hard drives, CDs, zip disks, etc.) that are no longer accessible through current technologies.

Being able to transfer the files to appropriate storage is only the first step. The archivist then needs to be able to open them to assess their content. Obsolete file formats sometimes cannot be opened or executed using current software. Older versions capable of opening the files might require specific environments (operating systems and hardware) to run. Copyright restrictions and the terms of software licenses may make it difficult or impossible for staff to locate versions they can legally use. In addition, digital objects accessed through more modern systems often render differently than they did in their original environment. The formatting or appearance may be altered,

and sometimes the behavior or even the actual content will change. Without the ability to access the content of older digital objects, it is difficult to determine which digital materials are most important and how best to allocate resources among collections. Given these challenges, nearly three quarters of respondents reported that their institutions store at least some of their legacy media as is, without transferring to new media or to server storage.

Collection donors have used a very wide variety of hardware and software configurations over time. As one respondent noted, "Each new collection seems to bring new technical issues that must be dealt with." In most libraries, it is unclear who should be responsible for developing technical solutions for accessing legacy media and obsolete file formats. This work is often outside the mandate of the information technology division and usually beyond the expertise of special collections staff. Some libraries and archives are creating "ingest labs" in house (the Bodleian Library, the British Library, Stanford, and the University of Virginia have working labs that serve as potential models). Others are outsourcing file recovery. An alternative file management strategy is to use a tool such as the Catweasel universal floppy disk controller, which is designed to connect legacy floppy disk drives to modern computer systems so that data can be read and written to floppy disks.

Interestingly, few respondents discussed challenges associated with complex digital objects (comprising more than one file and/or more than one file type), social media, digital objects stored in the cloud, websites, and networks of information, presumably, because most special collections and archives are just beginning to work with these types of digital objects.

The second category of ingest challenges relates to the workflows and systems needed to manage the digital objects once they are transferred off of their original carrier media. Maintaining privacy and providing adequate security topped the list of concerns. Respondents called for privacy and security policies specific to digital objects that address donor concerns and that insure compliance with university policies and federal and state laws. They noted the need for secure storage and networking and for tightly controlled access to files that contain personally identifiable information. (See Kirschenbaum, *Digital Forensics*, pages 49–58 for additional discussion of privacy and security issues related to born-digital objects.)

Several respondents noted that archivists need to be able to dedicate more time to developing policies and conducting test pilots. The lack of clear policies and workflows can lead to inconsistent practices across collections and across the institution, and to inefficient resource allocation. Without consistent policies and procedures libraries cannot insure continued access to the born-digital objects. The PARADIGM project (Bodleian Library) and AIMS project both provide guidance in establishing policies and workflows. The BitCurator Project, led by the School of Information Science at the University of North Carolina at Chapel Hill and by the Maryland Institute for Technology in the Humanities at the University of Maryland, is building on these efforts. It will define and test a digital curation workflow, beginning at the point of encountering holdings that reside on removable media and ending with interaction with an end user.

The tools and systems used in the ingest process tend to be modular, and many were originally developed for use by other communities. For example, commercial forensics packages (which are very useful for browsing content and identifying personally identifiable information) were developed specifically for law enforcement. While the functionalities of these products have guided institutions in the development of workflows, they cannot be easily combined to meet the needs of the library and archives community. As one respondent noted, "There are several open-source and commercial products that can do pieces of the workflow, but as they are not designed to work together there are inefficiencies in stringing these workflows together." Another respondent added that "most ingest software is in alpha or beta release, with long-term roadmaps for future development." Early adopters and those libraries able to develop their own systems need to be comfortable with uncertainty and a certain amount of churn. Other archives are waiting for system development to catch up with their needs. Systems currently used include Archivematica, Rosetta, and the Curator's Workbench; others like Hypatia and BitCurator show potential for the future.

The final category of challenges related to ingest relates to the capacity needed to scale up workflows and systems to manage the flood of born-digital objects needing preservation. Respondents highlighted the need for sufficient storage space, adequate network capacity, increased staffing, staff training, automation of standard tasks, and enterprise-level systems. One respondent noted, "Our current archival storage was scaled to accommodate our analog to digital digitization program." It is more challenging to estimate the needs for born-digital special collections and archival materials: the timing for acquisitions can be hard to predict; the volume is not always known at the time of receipt (often because the digital objects are on legacy media); the formats often vary widely; and it is often unclear which materials will need to be restricted (because the files cannot be accessed before receipt due to media or format).

Storage Challenges

The challenges related to storage systems can be separated into three major areas: systems limitations, organizational challenges, and insufficient resources (i.e., not enough available space and high storage costs). The challenges surrounding systems limitations were divided between the need for preservation-quality infrastructure and the need for security for and access to the materials themselves. Organizational challenges fell into three categories: policy and planning, gaining and retaining sufficient staff and skills, and managing the organizational structure (from the department up to the entire organization) while maintaining effective coordination between all the stakeholders. One set of concerns about sufficient resources represents two sides of the same coin: insuring adequate file storage space and its cost. Other challenges related to storage space include the difficulty in estimating and predicting capacity needs. One comment that summarizes the issues well indicates that storage needs for born-digital records should not be only the responsibility of the library and archives: "Future storage needs for large-scale ingest of born-digital special collections materials will probably be integrated into university-wide planning for digital repositories, a digital asset management system, and networked storage and continuity planning."

Access Challenges

The biggest access and discovery challenge, described by 32 respondents, is the sensitivity of materials—concerns about copyright, confidentiality, privacy, intellectual property, and personally identifiable information. The second biggest challenge is IT infrastructure, or rather, the lack of it (28 respondents). Particular concerns in this area include user interface, the need to integrate multiple systems, and the ability to handle very large files. Other significant challenges are the need to develop policies, processes, and tools for arranging and describing born-digital materials in ways that make them most accessible, including the integration of description for digital and non-digital materials; rights management (restrictions specific to users rather than materials); and staff time and skills. Interestingly, *time* was twice as much of a concern for respondents as *staff skills*. This makes sense as more professionals are assigned responsibility for these materials and go on to develop the necessary skills, but *staff* may still mean the only person, or one of a very few, responsible for managing these types of materials at their institutions. The remaining concerns included metadata standardization, differing levels of donor restrictions and how to apply them in an online environment, format standardization and migration, and institutional support (including funding).

Respondents' concerns grow even more complex when restrictions on sensitive materials (those subject to copyright, confidentiality, privacy, and intellectual property concerns) are combined with rights management by user group and donor-imposed limitations on access, because each of these types of restrictions can vary from case to case. Reference desk staff have dealt with the complexity of access restrictions in face-to-face transactions for decades, but libraries lack automated systems that can do the same during online transactions where staff are not there to intervene.

Respondents' comments on registration procedures highlight the nature of this challenge. Most institutions that provide access to born-digital materials are either doing so in their reading rooms and following standard reading room registration procedures or are providing access to the materials online with no registration procedure. These limited approaches are directly linked to the second biggest access challenge for respondents, the lack of a fully developed IT infrastructure for delivering born-digital materials to researchers. Other technology concerns include user interface design, the need to navigate multiple disconnected systems, and problems supporting large file sizes.

Providing access to archival materials is, of course, dependent on appropriate arrangement and description, and so it should be no surprise that many respondents stated a need to further develop policies, processes, and tools for arranging and describing born-digital materials in ways that make them most accessible, including the integration of description for born-digital, digitized, and non-digital materials.

The survey results indicate that our profession is moving towards a higher comfort level with the standardization of both metadata and file formats. Furthermore, institutional support is a challenge at only three institutions, which would seem to illustrate administrators' growing understanding of the need to support access to born-digital materials. Possible areas for future research include the use of analytics and user studies to track the quantitative and qualitative aspects of access to these materials by off-site researchers and the challenges of providing not just basic access but value-added reference services to those users.

Privacy Concerns

The survey team was surprised that most respondents did not address the potential institutional liability posed by personally identifiable information (PII) within born-digital materials, beyond the imposition of access restrictions. (PII includes information such as social security numbers, credit card numbers, logins, passwords, PINs, and medical and financial records.) Seventy-one percent of respondents indicated that their gift agreements did not include language that acknowledged born-digital materials. While ownership transfer, copyright, and some standard restrictions can be handled through the traditional deed of gift, gaining permission from the donor to use forensic tools that allow recovery and review of deleted files while searching for PII is not a standard option. Since such actions might alter donated files or uncover files not intended for transfer, requesting permission through the gift agreement or some other policy document is highly recommended.

While 71% of respondents have policies regarding whether files with PII should be retained with restrictions or destroyed, only 43% have policies indicating whether born-digital materials can be made available for research use before they are screened for PII. One respondent's comment that "all special collections materials have personally identifiable information (PII)" is quite true. However, paper-based collections have always benefited from security through obscurity. There is no fast or easy way to uncover social security and credit card numbers in paper-based collections. With born-digital records, on the other hand, there are many tools available that can search and locate PII, even in deleted or hidden files. Such content, improperly managed, not only puts the file creator at risk, but also may be in violation of an institution's security and privacy policy for this type of information. Eighty percent of respondents indicated that they do not have a written PII policy. Greater security is needed for unscreened born-digital records, especially if they are stored on networked servers.

Conclusion

The responses to this survey indicate that many ARL libraries and archives have begun working with born-digital materials in their collections, despite the fact that enterprise level systems and best practices for managing these materials in an archival setting are still in development, and despite concerns that they do not have the resources to scale their work to meet current and future demand. This willingness to experiment, to learn new skills, and to seek to understand the scope of the issues is building expertise within the library and archives profession, and has insured access to some born-digital holdings, at least in the near term. It also signals a shift from a wait-and-see attitude to a more empowered something-is-better-than-nothing approach to managing born-digital materials.

Respondents identified the following as critical for transitioning their work with born-digital materials from projects to programs:

- Collaborative solutions for dealing with hardware and software obsolescence.
- More, and more appropriate, storage for born-digital materials (long-term, authenticated, secure, verified, backed-up, and geographically distributed). As one respondent noted, "Archives are guaranteed preservation only if stored on enterprise data storage."
- Automation of as much of the workflow as possible.
- Asset-level access control to enable tiered access to restricted records.

Many institutions are working with digitized content or licensed digital content and are only now beginning to explore the ways in which born-digital, primary-source materials may be different. For example, it is difficult to estimate storage needs for born-digital primary sources stored on legacy media prior to accessioning and processing them. Privacy concerns are magnified when large bodies of easily searchable digital material may contain personally identifiable information. The workflows and infrastructure built for digitized content are often insufficient for born-digital primary sources.

While some special collections rely on a single staff member to manage all aspects of preserving and providing access to born-digital materials, more frequently staff from special collections, library IT, digital repositories, digital curation, and other areas work together to ingest, appraise, describe, preserve, and provide access to this content. The distributed nature of this model allows the library to leverage existing expertise, but it may also mean that no one has the big picture. These situations make it difficult to track the resources needed to manage the materials—which then makes it difficult to estimate current and future costs. Distributed responsibility can also threaten the long-term survival of the materials, either when no one feels empowered to make decisions or when someone makes decisions without having all of the relevant information. Staff need models of existing teams that describe how responsibilities are assigned and decisions are made collaboratively.

Survey responses indicate that best practices will take some time to develop: infrastructure, systems, and tools are in development; libraries continue to experiment with organizational models to find those that will be most effective to manage born-digital, primary-source materials; and the variety of record formats continues to grow. While several libraries and archives have developed scalable solutions that work within their own context, few of the solutions developed to date have been transferable between institutions. Waiting for time-tested systems and practices, however, is not an option. For now we need to settle for "good enough" practice and continue to invest time and resources in developing systems and workflows that will prevent a "digital dark age" for the first part of the 21st century.

SURVEY QUESTIONS AND RESPONSES

The SPEC survey on Managing Born-digital Special Collections and Archival Materials was designed by **Naomi Nelson**, Director of the David M. Rubenstein Rare Book & Manuscript Library, and **Seth Shaw**, Electronic Records Archivist, at Duke University; **Cynthia Ghering**, director of the University Archives and Historical Collections, and **Lisa Schmidt**, Electronic Records Archivist, at Michigan State University; **Michelle Belden**, Access Archivist and IT Coordinator for the Special Collections Library, **Jackie R. Esposito**, University Archivist and Head, Records Management Services, and **Tim Pyatt**, Dorothy Foehr Huck Chair and Head of the Eberly Family Special Collections Library, at Pennsylvania State University; and **Nancy Deromedi**, head of the Digital Curation division, and **Michael Shallcross**, Assistant Archivist, in the Bentley Historical Library at the University of Michigan. These results are based on data submitted by 64 of the 126 ARL member libraries (51%) by the deadline of March 26, 2012. The survey's introductory text and questions are reproduced below, followed by the response data and selected comments from the respondents.

The 2010 OCLC Research report, *Taking Our Pulse*, listed management of born-digital materials as the biggest challenge facing libraries, special collections, and archives, after space and facilities concerns. Over the last decade the materials acquired for our libraries, archives, and manuscript collections were very likely created as digital objects that may or may not have analog surrogates. If modern special collections and archives are to stay relevant and continue to provide access to unique and authentic records, ARL libraries need to manage and preserve born-digital materials, which for the purposes of this survey include institutional records, author's drafts on floppy discs, digital photographs and moving images, and electronic theses and dissertations, among others. It excludes commercial products such as e-journals.

This survey explores the tools, workflow, and policies special collections and archives staff use to process, manage, and provide access to born-digital materials they collect. It also looks at which staff process and manage born-digital materials and how they acquire the skills they need for these activities, and how libraries have responded to the challenges that managing born-digital materials present.

BACKGROUND

1. Does your library currently collect and manage born-digital materials? N=64

Yes	59	92%
No, but we plan to	5	8%
No, and we have no plans to	0	—

STAFFING

If collecting born-digital materials is in the planning stages, please answer the following questions to the best of your ability based on plans at this time.

2. Please indicate how many staff are (will be) charged with collecting and managing born-digital materials at your library. Include both the number of FTEs and number of individuals. N=60

	Minimum	Maximum	Mean	Median	Std Dev
FTE	0.10	60	4.73	2.00	9.25
Individuals	1.00	48	6.64	5.50	7.75

Please enter any additional comments you have about the staff who collect and manage born-digital materials. N=47

Special Collections/Archives

All curators and archivists could potentially collect born-digital materials, so I'm including all of them!

All staff who are currently responsible for paper records will/have responsibilities for managing born-digital materials.

Digital Records Archivist (full time), University Archivist, and two curators.

Four full-time professional curators collect born-digital materials along with analog materials and a wide variety of other duties. We have no dedicated field collectors.

In addition, we have one student (.25 FTE) and another part-time intern.

Our University Archivist is our point person for born-digital material.

Right now we have a full time Digital Archivist in our Film and Media Archive, and a staff member in University Archives who has 50% of her job designated for digital collections. I would anticipate needing to add more staff capacity for this in other units of the department.

The breakdown of FTE hours to staff above reflects one person, the Digital Archivist, working solely on collecting and managing born-digital materials as well as 5 other staff members spending part of their time to reach the equivalent of 2.0 FTE. These numbers do not include those outside of the special collections unit, such as in preservation, technical services, and IT units, who help to develop systems like repositories and catalogs that help manage these materials.

There are currently two individuals in our Special Collections Department who play (and will continue to play) a key role in collecting and managing born-digital materials, but given the primary responsibilities of these individuals, their time (collectively) does not constitute even a single FTE.

Digital Curation/Repository Staff

Although we are collecting and managing born-digital materials, there are not specific job descriptions within the archives that are related to such activities. Working with born-digital content is under the purview of archivists and select staff. The library does have a digital preservation coordinator but that position addresses only select parts of managing born-digital content.

Archives and Digital Collections both expect to have a role in managing these materials.

We have one professional managing our institutional repository.

We have three collection areas for our repository where we collect and manage born-digital materials. The core collections manager works with scholarly resources (ETDs, faculty deposits, and general collections), as well as providing oversight for all born-digital collections. The Digital Archivist oversees Special Collections/University Archives collections. The research collection manager manages research data. The research associate (new position) assists him with faculty outreach and collection building. Research data is a rapidly growing area for born-digital materials. The Digital Data Curator sets digital preservation standards and manages the ingest, durability, and security of all digital collections and the Digital Projects Coordinator oversees the workflow of all digital collection building. None of these positions works exclusively with born-digital materials, but all work with some percentage of born-digital materials. We estimate that born-digital resources represent approximately 20–25% of our current collection ingest. We have many positions that create metadata and develop tools for the repository but they are not specifically tasked with collecting and managing born-digital materials.

Various units/unit not specified

Arts Library has 2 FTE plus 2 students at 25%; Research Data Curation figures include both librarians who work on collections and technology staff who build the storage and discovery applications.

Currently .5; plan to hire one FTE this year, and train an existing FTE the following year. So the above reflects this.

Includes Electronic Records Archivists, Digital Curation Librarian, IT Staff.

Institutional Repository (IR) Coordinator, Digital Humanities Librarian, staff in the Digital Development and Web Services Unit, staff in the Digital Library Center within the Digital Services and Shared Collections Department, and faculty and staff in the Special and Area Studies Collections Department.

It is difficult for us to break out FTEs for this work, as it is generally integrated with other work. For example, our Records Manager is responsible for working with digital content from the university; our Digital Initiatives Librarian works with born-digital as well as digitized content, etc. We also have three people outside special collections areas that spend a portion of their time working with electronic theses and dissertations; they are not included in this figure.

Most of the staff involved with these projects participate less than full-time. Group includes librarians, technicians, developers, and project managers.

Nearly all staff members have some responsibility for digital materials, but only as part of their job. Estimate is therefore very rough. One staff member is oriented predominantly toward digital.

No one staff member is charged solely with this responsibility. Rather, all professional staff who have a role in acquiring new collections also have the responsibility to undertake these tasks.

One FTE is for the Director of Research Systems Development, who is not a Special Collections staff member but manages the Institutional Repository where the dark archives are located. Another is for non-Special Collections staff who manage the instance of CONTENTdm, which includes accessible born-digital materials.

One staff member is tasked with developing and maintaining the born-digital accession workflow process, all staff work with born-digital content in some capacity in the arrangement and description process.

Only one of these positions is devoted full-time to managing/collecting digital special collections materials.

Over the next few years, we hope to increase to 3 FTE (2 FTE permanent staff and 1 FTE project staff or interns).

Responsibility for collecting and managing born-digital materials is currently shared by librarians and archivists with responsibilities for special collections, university archives, geospatial data, ETDs, cataloguing & metadata. The library will soon hire a Digital Special Collections Librarian who will take the lead on collecting and managing born-digital special collections. This will lead to a higher FTE number than reported here.

Staff include University Archives personnel, the Faculty of Medicine Archivist, Libraries Collections Management personnel, the University Records Manager, Libraries IT personnel, and contract metadata technicians.

The Libraries have recently reorganized, still in process of figuring this out.

The numbers above speak to departments with particular responsibility for the management and long-term support for digital files, not for the collection development aspect. Collection development of born-digital materials will be carried out by curatorial and archivist staff not reflected in these numbers.

The staff are not dedicated only to this activity but it falls under the scope of other archival work.

There is no one person who does this full time. Everyone involved is focused on this issue as part of all of their other duties.

These individuals are not devoted exclusively to born-digital materials, but born-digital materials will invariably be part of the collections these individuals acquire, organize, preserve, and describe. The Head of Special Collections and Archives collects archival materials, which increasingly include born-digital materials. The Archivist is responsible for arranging and describing archival materials, including born-digital materials. The Digital Project Specialist assists the Head of SCA and the Archivist in acquiring, storing, preserving, describing, migrating, and providing access to these files. The Digital Projects Specialist administers the various digital repositories that preserve and provide access to these materials as well.

These numbers are very difficult to accurately compile. Most staff members do not have hard time allocations for born-digital materials. Most staff members do not have explicit job descriptions regarding born-digital materials. Also, those staff who do have allocations or explicit job descriptions may also be responsible for other tasks.

This includes metadata experts, digital curation staff, and repository services.

This question is difficult to answer with any accuracy. We currently collect very little born-digital materials and we have no one individual that is dedicated to this task or will be dedicated to it within the foreseeable future. Almost all of our special collections receive a small amount of born-digital materials and therefore the staff that is "charged" with managing and collecting the materials are no different than those that collect our paper-based materials.

This will be part of everyone's responsibilities.

This will become a component of the work of each of our four archivists responsible for acquiring all archival materials, regardless of format.

Two staff in Special Collections collect and manage born-digital content. In our Scholarly Publishing and Data Management team we have five individuals who are managing digital content.

We are at the earliest stages of formulating a formal strategy for ingesting born-digital Special Collections content. The figures provided above are a best guess as to how many people may be involved and makes the following assumption: University Archives staff member (0.25 FTE), Manuscripts Division Staff member (0.25 FTE), Programmer/Analyst (0.25 FTE), Metadata Specialist (0.75 FTE).

We do not have a full-time person, and since we are doing this on an ad-hoc basis now, the quarter FTE is really just a guestimate. I, through my curatorial duties, and our digital services librarian handle it.

We have 60% time of two people (both professional staff), roughly half the time of one software engineer, and a small amount of time from a core services/Mac specialist team member.

We have added these duties to the work of the Technical Services Archivist.

We have numerous staff who are involved with managing or collecting born-digital, but none of these positions are dedicated full time to the activities.

We have three FTE staff who have some responsibility to manage born-digital content in some capacity in their job descriptions: Archivist, Digital Projects and Outreach Digital Assets Librarian (currently conducting job search to fill this role), Digital Initiatives Librarian.

Work falls into three general areas: web archiving, electronic archives, and audio and video oral history interviews.

3. **Please indicate which strategy your library has used or plans to use to address staffing needs for processing and/or managing born-digital materials. Check all that apply. N=63**

Add responsibilities for born-digital materials to current positions	59	94%
Create new staff positions	29	46%
Recast an existing position dedicated to managing born-digital materials	23	37%
Hire interns for born-digital materials projects	15	24%
Hire consultants/contractors for born-digital materials projects	9	14%
Other staffing strategy	13	21%

Please describe the other staffing strategy. N=13

Also hoping to work with staff from larger library who are charged with managing born-digital NON special collections.

As the library makes strategic hires in other areas (e.g., Digital Repository Coordinator), we will attempt to include electronic records expertise in the desired skill sets.

Budget for staff in grant-supported digital preservation projects.

Capitalize on existing expertise to leverage capacity where it exists.

IT Specialists are being used. Currently Still Pictures just add responsibilities for born-digital materials to current positions. Electronic records preservation staff directly contribute to the Electronic Records Archive activities. Considerable workload has increased pertaining to system design, development, testing, and analysis.

May link up with other units in the Libraries or beyond.

One librarian has had his position expanded to include acquisition and management of gaming collections.

Recast an existing position to include managing born-digital materials.

The e-records/digital resources archivist position that is split with the office of the CIO does investigate tools and provides advice to curators and curatorial staff in more effective ways of accessioning and managing born-digital materials.

Trained high-level students dedicated to born-digital projects (4 students).

We expect there will be a need to create new positions and/or recast existing positions for managing born-digital materials.

We have a newly created digital resources library unit that will work with born-digital.

We have created new staff positions. The Digital Archivist, a position in the Special Collections/University Archives Unit, manages digital collection building for that unit. The Digital Project Coordinator position was created to add oversight and accountability to the many digital collection-building projects underway. We repurposed a position to become the Digital Data Curator, and another position to become the repository Digital Collections Manager. We added responsibilities for digital collection management to an existing professional position, the Social Sciences Data Librarian. We are actively working with other library liaisons to build digital collection building into their service repertoire. We hope to add an electronic records management position in the next 1 to 2 years in Special Collections/University Archives, to manage the official electronic records of the university. This position will work with an ER system, rather than with the repository although we anticipate sharing born-digital materials from the ER system that have scholarly value and are available for open access use across the two systems.

4. **What opportunities does your library pursue (or plan to pursue) to increase staff expertise in managing born-digital materials? Check all that apply. N=64**

Conference attendance	58	91%
On-the-job training	58	91%
Training provided by professional organizations	57	89%
SAA workshop/Summer Camp attendance	41	64%
Independent study	39	61%
Local courses in computer or digital technology	21	33%
Training provided by vendors	15	23%
Rare Book School attendance	14	22%
ARMA workshop attendance	8	13%
Other opportunity	9	14%

Please specify the other opportunity. N=9

Anything we can get!

CURATEcamp (curatecamp.org)

Mentoring

METRO, NYART; also engagement with groups such as PASIB, LibDevConX; webinars from DuraSpace and NISO; discussions with colleagues from other institutions, especially Cornell.

Peer-to-peer on-the-job training

Regional meetings such as the Northwest Archivists, also the Northwest Digital Archives part of the Orbis Cascade Alliance.

Vendors in this case refers to training conducted by our prime ERA contractor (Lockheed Martin, in 2009 and 2010). On the job training: "We all help each other as we learn about the utility of new software tools, skills, and techniques in processing digital images." Several staff have participated in electronic records management courses conducted in field locations.

We are currently teaching an in-house course on research data management for library faculty liaisons, metadata librarians, and library technologists. The emphases are on understanding the nature of research data, metadata, rights and privacy, and data curation, with a goal to building project teams to work effectively together on research data management. This is not exclusive to born-digital content, but we are finding most of our research data is born digital.

Workshops/Institute such as DigCCurr; CurateCamp; Digital Preservation Management Workshop.

BORN-DIGITAL MATERIALS COLLECTED

5. Which of the following categories of born-digital materials does your library currently collect or plan to collect? Check all that apply. N=64

	Currently Collect	Plan to Collect	N
Personal archives such as email, photographs, documents, calendars, etc.	46	13	59
Organizational or institutional archives	41	18	59
University/institutional records	44	13	57
Electronic theses and dissertations	54	4	58
Research data	21	28	49
Non-commercial e-only publications	30	11	41
Learning content and course management systems	8	11	19
Other category	18	—	18
Number of Responses	64	41	64

If you selected "Other category" above, please briefly describe the other category of born-digital materials your library currently collects or plans to collect. N=17

Publications/related materials

Academic department newsletters, documentation from university research centers

Commercial e-only publications through copyright deposit and purchase/subscriptions. As part of our manuscript collection efforts we do collect materials from individuals. Donations, gifts, and exchange items are another channel for acquisition.

Currently collect commercial e-only publications.

Digitized books, campus websites, campus journals, etc.

AV/Research data

Faculty portfolios, campus video productions, oral histories

I included theses, research data, and content management systems even though they are the province of the larger university library system, not special collections. Our collections in all areas are very small, perhaps just a few items as test cases, and in some cases, simply being stored on drives counts as collection.

Oral histories

Oral history video/audio interviews

Research data is still an unclear area, in part simply defining "research data" is difficult. Re: course management material, that area is also unclear.

Scholar curated archives and research materials in the humanities, often referred to as capta instead of data to recognize that the data is not discrete/quantitative, but data as it is captured/presented; born-digital materials from other GLAM (galleries, libraries, archives, and museums); oral histories; web archiving.

Born-digital audio and video oral histories created at the university. May collect social media from institutions/individuals whose archives we hold.

ETDs/Student works

Other types of student works

Outside of ETDs what we collect born-digital is currently minimal—some university records, an e-pub, and undergraduate honor theses. However, ETDs and honor theses do not come under the curatorial purview of Special Collections and Archives.

Other

Maps, catalog indices

Thematically related websites, e.g., in the areas of human rights, historic preservation/urban planning, religion/theology, and personal websites for individuals whose archives we hold.

We are the custodians of the electronic Presidential records transferred to NARA at the end of each administration. While Presidential records will remain the vast majority of our electronic holdings we also have small volumes of personal electronic records that will need a more systematic management approach in the coming years.

We currently access records and fonds that include born-digital material, mostly on media such as hard drives, floppy disks, and CDs.

Websites, blogs, etc.

Additional Comments

Content support born-digital publications and artworks.

Electronic theses and dissertations, research data, and non-commercial e-only publications are handled through the Institutional Repository, which is not part of Special Collections.

Research data: initiatives in this area are currently managed by the Research Data Management Service Group within the University Library, not within special collections units.

6. **Which of the following types of born-digital materials does your library currently collect or plan to collect? Check all that apply. N=64**

	Currently Collect	Plan to Collect	N
Audio recordings (including podcasts)	49	14	63
Photographs	53	9	62
Moving images	42	19	61
Video recordings	48	13	61
Texts (such as unstructured office documents)	43	12	55
Institutional websites	24	28	52
Email	23	23	46
Databases	21	20	41
Other types of websites	18	20	38
Geographical Information Systems (GIS) data	19	12	31
Social media (e.g., institutional Facebook pages, Twitter accounts)	6	23	29
Executable files	14	4	18
Enterprise systems data	2	13	15
Computer games	5	5	10
Other type	6	6	12
Number of Responses	62	49	64

If you selected "Other type" above, please briefly describe the other type(s) of born-digital materials your library currently collects or plans to collect. N=12

Currently Collect

Excel spreadsheets

Illustrator, InDesign files (design production files), iMovie project files

Music scores. Outside of Special Collections, the institutional repository collects born-digital moving images, video recordings, databases, texts, executable files, and GIS.

Posters and other graphic materials in digital form

Serials and monographs

Plan to Collect

Any materials we've collected in the past that are now in an electronic format.

Architectural design files (e.g., CAD)

Because we collect archival material from a variety of external people and organizations, it is difficult to predict exactly what formats of born-digital material we may acquire in the future.

Much of this territory is still in discussion.

Oral histories

Research datasets

Additional Comments

Research data in various formats (.csv, XML, tab delimited, etc.)

INGEST POLICIES AND PROCEDURES

7. Has your library developed language for your gift/purchase agreements that is specific to born-digital content? N=63

Yes	18	29%
No	45	71%

Answered Yes

Archives does not distinguish between traditional and digital records in this document. Our copyright statement is inclusive of born-digital and digitized material.

Gift agreement includes a note regarding electronic records and requires the donor to agree that there are no other copies of the e-records available elsewhere.

Gift agreements acknowledge the possibility despite the fact that it is not clear to me or our counsel why special mention is necessary.

Language for gifts/purchases that include digital content is developed on a case-by-case basis.

Only for ETDs. Nothing yet for general donations of born-digital materials.

Only when applicable to the collection.

The language is an optional add-on to the existing donor agreements.

We have specific language in some of our agreements, but we have not yet standardized the language or created a set of standard language that can be used for born-digital collections. We are working on standardizing our approach.

Answered No

But we are currently drafting such language.

In general, we feel that our regular agreements will cover most issues related to born-digital content. In the cases where this is not the case we will customize these agreements to address specific issues.

In process of developing.

No, we are "media independent" in our deeds.

Our current licenses cover both digitally converted and born-digital content.

Our gift agreements already encompass most issues pertaining to the management of born-digital content, but not language specific to born-digital content.

Our intake of born-digital materials is still small and is often linked with traditional analog collections.

Revision of gift/purchase agreements will be one focus area of the new Digital Special Collections Librarian.

So far, only ad hoc language for a single born-digital archival collection.

The agreement language has not yet been finalized, but it will be updated to reflect areas that were not as relevant to paper materials.

This does need to be addressed for reasons of preservation/migration and also online access.

We did develop a special deed of gift for project involving solicitation of images and other born-digital content from the community, because we were concerned that the casual way in which we were likely to receive content would reduce our chances of getting donors to sign our standard form. Whether born-digital content is more likely to be donated casually (i.e., the digital equivalent of being left on the doorstep) is hard to say at this point; if it is, then this was an adaptation to that quality.

We have amended some specific deeds of gift to allow for electronic publication of born-digital content, but this is very rare so far.

We have begun the discussions to consider how to include those revisions.

We will be addressing this in the near future.

Working on gift agreement to include all types of media, including born-digital content.

8. Has your library developed workflows for the ingest and processing of born-digital materials? N=64

Yes	36	56%
No	28	44%

If yes, please briefly describe any models or examples you found most helpful as you developed your workflow.

Models/Examples

Currently using Google Spreadsheet APIs for ingestion, but interested in approaches such as SWORD and BagIt.

Digital Curation Centre lifecycle model

Examples provided by the Digital Preservation Management Workshop at Cornell.

Inspiration for this process came from UT Austin's digital preservation work (https://pacer.ischool.utexas.edu/handle/2081/21808) and Stanford's digital forensics work (http://lib.stanford.edu/digital-forensics), as well as the steps and validation processes in Archivematica and Duke Data Accessioner (though we are not currently using these tools).

Model(s) that were helpful to Preservation staff in developing workflows for ingest and processing born-digital records was the Open Archival Information reference model and the Digital Curation Center model.

Models we have used include documentation from Stanford and the Bodleian, as well as microservices as described by Archivematica

OAIS, IDEALS

PARADIGM; Existing accessions process for analog materials.

The AIMS project, specifically Stanford's work on digital forensics.

The most useful examples are real-world use cases for the full process of how to support the ingest, normalization, preservation, and access of born-digital files within a full repository and digital library system.

We are in the process of creating our workflows for ingest and processing. We have some workflows now that will soon change as our repository infrastructure evolves. Models we have used include documentation from Stanford and the Bodleian, as well as microservices as described by Archivematica.

We have studied and learned from the Duke Data Accessioner, the PARADIGM project in the UK, the OAIS model, and professional literature in developing our workflow.

We participated in the AIMS project and have developed a model for ingest from media following a forensics model. We are also utilizing forensics tools to enable arrangement and description.

We referenced many models while developing our own. Primarily, our workflow is based on the work we undertook as part of the Born-Digital Archives: An Inter-Institutional Model for Stewardship (AIMS) grant. That project in turn synthesized many research projects and workflows, but was heavily influenced by the following projects and tools: PARADIGM, OAIS, futureArch, Digital Lives, InterPARES, TAPER, SALT, the work of Chris Prom on his Practical E-Records blog and report to, Archivematica, Curator's Workbench, work on the Salman Rushdie Papers at Emory University, PLANETS.

Work by Seth Shaw and Ben Goldman in conference presentations on practical approaches to born-digital collections at the Midwest Archives Conference and the Society of American Archivists. Duke Data Accessioner. Chris Prom's blog. CIC electronic records policy guidelines. MetaArchive and ICPSR's guidelines on development of digital preservation policies. Specifications of processes/tools/procedures from Archivematica, California Digital Library's Merritt, MetaArchive, etc. Publications from NDIIPP, ICPSR, InterPARES, PREMIS, etc.

Workflow Descriptions

A procedure to receive digital images and assign file names according to local directory needs is in place. Scripts for ingesting ETDs from ProQuest. Ad hoc scripting to structure and ingest research data.

Currently the workflow is very straightforward and is intended to protect the records against loss due to failure of the information carrier.

One principal driver for us was compliance with the requirements of the Presidential Records Act (PRA). The PRA gives the Archivist legal custody of all Presidential records at the point of an administration transition. The PRA also obligates NARA to respond to access requests to those records immediately after we receive custody (public access requests begin five years after transition; in the first five years we respond to special access requests). To meet both these circumstances our workflows have to account for the ingest of a large volume of holdings in as short a time frame as possible while giving us search and access capabilities to support asset-level review and production of copies of the electronic records for external requesters. Model(s) that were helpful to Preservation staff in developing workflows for ingest and processing born-digital records was the Open Archival Information reference model and the Digital Curation Center model. In Still Pictures, we have a multi-page set of basic instructions that cover what processing is, but essentially we: 1) obtain the digital images from the agency usually by downloading onto media for transfer to NARA. 2) Once here we make a copy for OPA processing. 3) Processing accession for ERA involves reviewing images to delete those that are temporary; ensuring unique filenames for images; appending our RG and series designations to each digital image; when images do not have captions, appending whatever information is available to each image in a folder; reviewing the metadata to make sure there is a link to the individual images; if caption information is in header, copying that out into a separate text file if needed. Depending on the condition of the accession, there may be many other processing steps needed to make it ERA and OPA ready. 4) Go thru the laborious process of ingesting the accession into ERA. 5) Complete processing for OPA and work with NPOL to get the images uploaded to OPA for reference use.

Our process is still being developed and tested. Currently it includes the following elements: Capture, metadata/content extraction. FTKImager to capture disk image, generate disk/file level metadata and checksums, and extract content directory from disk. BASH shell script to combine and organize disk image and metadata files. File Characterization/ Normalization JHOVE and/or DROID for characterization/validation. FileMerlin to convert/normalize legacy text files. Adobe Acrobat to migrate text files to PDF/A. Appraisal, organization, and description (akin to traditional archival processing). Human uses Excel spreadsheet to record appraisal decisions, organize content, and enter descriptive metadata. Ingest XSLT used on Excel spreadsheet to package the digital files and create Dublin Core .xml metadata files for ingest into our DSpace repository. Command line batch ingest to DSpace.

Our workflows are not specific to born-digital materials. For electronic records management, we have record schedules and retention policies that apply equally to analog, digitized, and born-digital records. For the digital repository, we utilize a workflow management system that enables us to establish collections, develop and document master file formats, validate and document technical characteristics of files, develop metadata, attach digital files to metadata, and create and ingest METS packages. None of this workflow is specific to born-digital content but works equally well with digital and born-digital content.

We have different workflows for different content types. All workflows are preliminary and evolving.

We have implemented Archivematica as a key element in our accessions workflow.

We have localized workflows for some of our materials (e.g., EDTs), and are looking at methods for managing ingest in a more distributed or decentralized manner.

Workflow for our theses & dissertations: students submit electronically through a web form in our DSpace repository and there are two levels of validation by people afterwards within the repository before it is published. We used workflow models from other universities when setting our own.

Workflows in Development

In process of developing.

In process of development as library; VRA workflow model used by art image library.

There are some workflows in place, however, they are in the process of being reviewed and modified/expanded.

This is a work in progress.

This is in the midst of change. Based on a preservation repository model. Current challenge is the model for collections being processed and what to do until they are processed.

Training the campus photographers to add some of their images into a CONTENTdm system hosted by the library.

We are currently in the process of creating these workflows and hope to have them implemented by the end of the 2012 calendar year.

We are currently in the process of creating these workflows with a vendor.

We are experimenting with ingest into DSpace. Very early stages.

We are in the midst of developing proper ingest procedures: some parts worked out, some not so much.

We are in the midst of developing such workflows. However, we are building the infrastructure to support these initiatives from the ground up and do not anticipate being able to ingest significant quantities of born-digital content for at least a year.

We are in the process of developing workflows.

Workflows and policies still in development. Waiting for sufficient, *secure* storage infrastructure.

Workflows are in development.

9. **Does your library currently ingest born-digital records stored on legacy media? N=64**

Yes	49	77%
No, but we plan to	12	19%
No, and we have no plans to	3	5%

10. Which of the following strategies does your library employ when ingesting born-digital records stored on legacy media? Check all that apply. N=60

	Current Strategy	Planned Strategy	N
Storing legacy media as is (without transfer to new media or server storage and/or keeping it with analog collection)	47	1	48
Developing a collection of legacy hardware that can be used to retrieve data from legacy media (e.g., 5.25" floppy drives, zip drives, etc.)	27	10	37
Outsourcing the process of retrieving the data from legacy media	15	20	35
Building new systems that replicate the function of the legacy systems (e.g., emulation, virtual systems)	8	9	17
Participating in a collaborative that is developing a collection of legacy hardware	3	8	11
Other strategy	13	9	22
Number of Responses	57	32	60

If you selected "Other strategy" above, please briefly describe the other strategy(ies) your library employs or plans to employ when ingesting born-digital records stored on legacy media. N=19

Current Strategy

A documented risk in our holdings is the presence of legacy media scattered throughout the textual holdings. We need a systematic means of accessing the data in these media to determine if the contents should be preserved as records in our holdings.

As new collections come in with digital content, we copy them to a server. Have not systematically gone back to find digital content in legacy collections, so those are being stored on legacy media.

Converting legacy files to modern file types.

For the most part, we are committed to access and will migrate files to the latest usable format to provide access to the content. We realize that we sacrifice the original look and feel of the files, as well as their functionality, but it is an acceptable loss given our main users for this content and the nature of our content so far (mostly word processing files). For example, when we have encountered legacy files on floppy disks, we have converted the files to the PDF-A format and made them accessible online. For materials with copyright or privacy concerns, these are available in a Virtual Reading Room, so just like our physical reading room in Special Collections, researchers must fill out an application form and agree to our terms before entering the Virtual Reading Room online to access the content.

One strategy: Using earlier (Mac) models to open older files, movies, etc. Holding some old software OS9, earlier versions of iMovie.

Remove data from media ourselves when we are able.

Storage on servers in a "Dark Archives."

Transferring content from legacy media to server storage.

We are selectively copying born-digital files (mostly photography) to our servers for backup. We hope these in turn will be moved over to the digital repository for digital preservation actions.

We have a sophisticated digital video encoding platform that enables us to retrieve video and audio data from a range of legacy formats (VHS, Digi Beta, etc.) For formats we cannot manage, such as reel-to-reel tapes, we occasionally outsource to a commercial vendor. Whether or not we retain the legacy media depends on whether it is accepted as a collection in our Special Collections/University Archives Department. If not, we return the legacy material to the collection owner. We are increasingly receiving research data in commercial formats such as Excel. Our current strategy is to document the version and test sample data with new software versions for backward compatibility and to store the data whenever possible in an alternative, less proprietary format. Currently, Excel and other database formats are also stored as CSV. We are looking at the DDI data format and other XML solutions as another non-proprietary standard. We are more interested in finding non-proprietary standards that retain the information content than in emulation or encapsulation of legacy data. Our biggest issues are research data formats proprietary to a specific data analysis tool, such as the FASTA format for gene sequencing, since we do not currently have an acceptable non-proprietary format for such data.

We have some legacy hardware but have no intention of building a true "collection." We use it to retrieve and transfer content from legacy media when possible. When we encounter a format we do not have hardware for, we turn to neighbor institutions for assistance; when this fails, we consider the likely value of the content on the legacy media. If it is not high, we will generally store the hardware as is. If it is high enough, we would consider outsourcing, dependent on cost and availability of funds.

We migrate digital media into a "digital archives" sever area that replicated our intellectual department divisions.

With some legacy media we can have our IT staff transfer the data, but I would not consider this outsourcing.

Planned Strategy

Migrate materials to newer media.

Plan to transfer data when resources are available.

Transfer to server storage (or, for example., repository).

Unknown. The planning process is just beginning.

We also have a strategy to investigate 3rd party vendors and their abilities for normalizing content for ingest.

We feel that the legacy hardware/software requirements for the digital content in our current "hybrid" collections are modest and can be addressed with local equipment. We have also purchased the "FRED" forensics system that will boost our capacity. We anticipate there will be some types of legacy media where we will need to use external vendors for content retrieval.

We plan to transfer records stored on legacy media to server storage and into the library's digital preservation repository. Two units are developing a collection of legacy hardware. One is outsourcing the process of retrieving the data.

Other Comments

We are currently pursuing a mix of 1, 2, and 4 but are interested in the fifth option and keeping track of collaborative efforts in the field.

We do not currently outsource the retrieval of born-digital materials from legacy media nor do we actively plan to, however, that doesn't rule out the possibility of doing so.

While we do not currently outsource the process of retrieving the data from legacy media, we have utilized this strategy in the past.

ETHICAL/APPRAISAL ISSUES

11. Below are ethical/appraisal issues that may be encountered while managing born-digital materials. Please indicate which of these issues are addressed by your library's ingest policies or procedures. Check all that apply. N=42

Whether to retain (under restriction) or destroy personally identifiable information (PII)	30	71%
Whether to preserve e-books, software, digital music, and other copyrighted content	20	48%
Whether to make files available for research use without having screened them for PII on the file level	18	43%
Whether to retain or destroy file fragments and deleted content in the absence of explicit guidance in the donor agreement	15	36%
Whether to preserve log files, preferences, browser caches and other types of ambient data in the absence of explicit guidance in the donor agreement	5	12%
Other issue	16	38%

Please describe the other issue. N=16

PII and Restricted Data

All special collections materials have personally identifiable information (PII). This may be different than sensitive information, which may be protected when PII cannot be.

Personal email, bills, contents of individual artists that we encountered.

Some records held by the Medical Center Archives contain Protected Health Information (PHI) and are covered under the HIPAA Privacy Rule.

There is an institute PII policy, but to my knowledge not a more formally written policy to specifically addresses managing archival materials.

We have policies that deal with copyrighted material regardless of medium and we have institutional policies that deal with PII and restricted data, but nothing that specifically applies to the collection of digital materials within the libraries.

While we have policies on privacy, we will need to develop more granular procedures for dealing with born-digital records that are in alignment with those policies.

Other issues

A variety of procedures are in place. Some address some of these issues; some do not.

All of these are covered by policies and procedures from across the Libraries, not just within the digital ingest group. As complex issues and concerns, these are not within any single policy and are instead supported by many policies and procedures.

Development of policy underway; donors have applied access restrictions.

Our holdings are unprocessed Presidential records that require access review and the completion of a notification process defined by Executive Order 13489 prior to public access to any of the records.

Related to appraisal, we are also trying to address whether or not this material is or will be deposited with another institution. Since the donor or depositor does not have to hand anything physically over to us, and even if they do, since they may easily make and retain a copy, we are concerned that we may be spending time and resources on material that is not unique and that the donor may wish to deposit in multiple institutions creating a redundant work to process the material in multiple places.

We are currently developing policies and procedures in this area in conjunction with the acquisition of our first major born-digital organizational archive.

We are in the process of creating policies for institutional records. These issues will primarily be addressed through file plans and retention schedules. We have not addressed these issues for personal materials.

We are just beginning to discuss these issues.

We have the ability to capture and maintain rights metadata, the IRB policies for specific research data. We can also control access to parts of a research data collection that need to be preserved but not made available for privacy or copyright issues. We hope to implement a dark archive in the coming year, but currently we will preserve born-digital resources that are in a fragile format (such as superseded video file formats).

We would follow existing guidelines from the print world, I expect. Hasn't come up yet.

12. **Does your library have a written policy that addresses your PII practice? N=59**

Yes	12	20%
No	47	80%

13. Please briefly describe up to three challenge(s) your library has faced in ingesting born-digital materials (e.g., file format, hardware, software, privacy or security issues, etc.) and how the library has addressed that challenge. N=60

Ingest Challenges Word Cloud

A significant challenge has to do with legacy media. The oldest format we have so far identified are 8" floppy disks in a WANG format (i.e., not a modern PC format). We also have identified a number of 5.25" and 3.5" floppy disks, as well as CD, DVD, and hard drive formats. We suspect that there also may be data tape formats in the stacks as well (an inventory project is currently underway), and have been in talks with a donor with data on IOMEGA jaz and zip disks. We have been able to acquire media to read the 5.25" and 3.5" floppy formats, but not the 8" formats. We have also acquired a forensic imaging device that can handle a number of data connector types such as SCSI, SATA, and IDE. When we are able to physically read a disk, some of these devices have controller cards or software that work only on specific operating systems, making it difficult sometimes to physically read disks in an efficient workflow (because some disks in a collection are read with one machine and one software, producing one kind of output file, while others need to be read on another machine using a different software and output file). For those pieces of media that we currently do not have hardware for, we have to evaluate the costs of acquiring the hardware against the value. For example, we could possibly find drives to read the 8" disks, but we are not guaranteed to find a controller card to make that drive compatible with a modern PC anyway. In this circumstance, we have therefore investigated the prices of having a vendor image the disks for us, but this also requires a cost-benefit analysis. Each disk contains less than 80 KB of data and the price just to image the disk is around $50 each. In addition, we need to ship the disks and we run the risk of having them lost or damaged in transport. As well, we would need to have some sort of confidentiality agreement with the vendor regarding the privacy of the data because we have no real idea of what is on the disk. After all of that, we could then send these disks to the vendor and find that they are unreadable anyway – there is no way to tell if a disk is readable until you attempt to read it. Finally, the issue of the scale of this legacy media is a challenge. We estimate currently that we hold less than 3,000 disks, but the time necessary just to load and transfer data from those disks is considerable. This is not even including the time it would take to process the materials as part of a collection, but simply to transfer it from the media where it is at a higher risk of corruption, to network storage. A second challenge related to the first, but separate, is the ability to actually read the data that is on the media. As described above, we have some material that is so old that it is not even readable by a modern computing system. Other data is not as old, but still presents significant problems with readability because the data is stored in file formats that are no longer compatible with modern operating systems or for which we simply don't have software to read. An example is architectural drawings created by a CAD software in the early 1990s. In this case we are able to work with our School of Architecture to locate some software to read these programs, but it does mean that we need to keep this software viable, which in many cases means running older operating systems or alternative operating systems to what we currently use on the forensic imaging hardware (which is primarily Windows). One of the pieces of software we have purchased is Forensic Tool Kit, which can identify and "read" thousands of file formats. However, these formats are primarily those that would be most commonly seen in criminal investigations, since that is what the software is designed for. So, things like CAD software from the early 90s are not included in their list of recognized formats. We have not seriously discussed trying to emulate any software or operating systems at this time, although we have watched with interest other projects that have done so. We do not view emulation as a viable approach at this time since our collections are so diverse and we do not have the type of technology staff in the library to really do this work efficiently. It would simply be impossible to have the resources available to emulate each and every program we are likely to encounter and to keep those emulations running in current environments. While there are some things we are likely to see a lot of (Microsoft Word documents, for example) we also feel that it is not worth the effort at this time to create an emulated environment when a migrated format (a PDF in this case) would be adequate. This is not to say that in the future emulation may not be attempted in special circumstances. A third very significant challenge is related to the lack of available tools for doing archival work with born-digital collections, as well as infrastructure in terms of repository and preservation networks that can meets the needs of access, management and preservation. There are several open-source and commercial products that can do pieces of the workflow, but as they are not designed to work together there are inefficiencies in stringing these workflows together. As an example, we use the Forensic Tool Kit software to extract some basic technical metadata, identify duplicate materials, and those that might contain predictable sensitive information such as SSNs or credit card numbers. The output of FTK, however, is some proprietary XML and a PDF report. We then use Archivematica to further extract technical details and establish a provenance through the creation of PREMIS metadata. We would then record information about a duplicate removed from the accession in Archivematica, but ingesting the duplicate file and then removing it manually per the FTK report. Finally, the PREMIS metadata record that Archivematica creates in nested inside a METS record for the entire accession. Our current storage network however, wants only the individual PREMIS records for each file, rather than the combined METS, so more work needs to be done to transfer the file between these two tools. Once the material goes through this network of tools, we still need to work on our repository and other digital asset management and discovery systems in order to suit the needs of this material which differs in many ways from the needs of other digital materials we store and manage such as e-books and –journals and digitized resources. This infrastructure needs to handle the preservation, management, access, and discovery of these materials. We are watching with interest the developments of open-source tools created by the archival community such as Archivematica, bitCurator, ArchivesSpace, and Curator's Workbench as well as potentially doing some work on the further development of Hypatia.

Adequate digital infrastructure to securely store and describe born-digital content. Adding these responsibilities onto existing staff: training, workload. No formal records management policy at the university.

Appropriately secure storage. Staffing resources. Policies and workflow development.

Copying/reformatting from old redundant file formats. Network latency and storage; lack of server space. Lack of software to support integrity of file reformatting.

Copyright: all our metadata contains a copyright statement for our digital object. Other options we can apply are banding and watermarking to objects. We include the copyright holder when it isn't our institution and we know who that is, but this becomes a challenge when unknown. In some instances, we have put up digitized objects, asking for input from our patrons for ownership. Fixity: we don't currently have a systematic way of guaranteeing fixity! We are actively working on a preservation plan that will address this issue. Authentication: we don't currently have a mechanism to authenticate born-digital objects – we "trust" the source and ingest. We are hoping to make this part of our Digitization Preservation Policy, which is currently in development.

Developing policies and procedures relating to the acquisition and ingest of born-digital content: the Digital Archivist has recently completed a research leave where he has drafted a digital preservation policy that could apply to born-digital materials. Developing an open-source digital asset management system: the ingest process for our digital asset management system has been unreliable in its early stages of development. The Libraries has dedicated an IT person to this system and has hired a vendor to further development of the system, particularly regarding its stability. Creating an inventory of born-digital material on legacy media: the Digital Archivist will soon be compiling such an inventory based on existing finding aids.

Developing secure hardware infrastructure to protect PII collected and retained; have worked closely with the campus IT security office. Securing secure, backed-up server space for dark archive. Planning access strategy for restricted content.

Digital storage space. We have recently conducted an inventory of all of our special collection digital assets (not just born-digital). This will be used to more effectively plan our storage needs—the amount and types of storage. Sustainability of digital library and preservation platform. We haven't yet adequately addressed this issue.

File format is an enormous challenge. We are receiving research data proprietary to specific data collection and analysis tools, such as the SURF surface mapping data produced by the software MountainsMap. Another is the gene sequencing data, FASTA, produced by the SOLiD gene sequencing system. We don't have non-proprietary formats in which to store this data and we don't know enough about persistence and backward compatibility for the tools. Our researchers are skilled at using the tools and interpreting the data but aren't able to answer our questions about persistence and longevity for the data. Thus far, our only strategy is to document the instruments that created the data, document as much as we know about the data (which is often in multiple files) and to bring this issue up in every research data gathering and suggest that conversations with these instrument providers are needed. File size is another challenge. Large files take a very long time to process and can make born-digital files difficult to manipulate in the repository and for end users to download. We currently bundle large files into zip files for downloading but need an effective background methodology for ingest.

File format on legacy tape drives from punch card data that has Census/private information for different nations. Need for old hardware on site for conversions and ingest with immediate time demands. Scaling up for the demand.

File formats: i.e., Word 1.0 documents. Hardware: i.e., receipt of records on 5 1/4" or 3 1/2" discs; no computers that will read such discs. Uncertainty about the authenticity of the records we have received. Do we have the only copy or are there multiple copies/versions available elsewhere?

Hardware and software. We don't always have the hardware and/or software to access legacy file formats, and don't know how to access files without changing their metadata. We try to collect obsolete hardware when possible, and sometimes outsource accessing these legacy files. Selection of file formats for streaming media; we are currently working on this with library IT staff. We face challenges trying to educate the university community about giving us their born-digital files, and lack confidence that we can preserve it and make it accessible because of lack of resources and internal technical expertise. We are working on outreach to university offices, and working on developing necessary skills for archiving born-digital content.

Hardware; lack of secure storage and backup. We are attempting to implement now, working with university IT. Privacy/security. We hope to develop written policies.

Images received in digital format but named idiosyncratically by the photographer. In order for these files to be used in a local digital environment it is necessary to provide meaningful file names in relation to existing or new local directories.

A procedure using a combination of Adobe Photoshop and Adobe Bridge was developed locally to batch process files to accomplish this task. Sensitive data: we have yet to work out issues surrounding born-digital institutional records with restricted access, e.g., promotion & tenure files, President's Office files, etc. An organization uses an online service to process applications that in the past had been delivered in paper format. Acquiring the records in a format that is useable by the archive may require a contract of some sort with the vendor. This remains to be resolved.

In 2010 the library acquired a collection of nearly 50 floppy discs and a number of CDs; most were unlabeled (or labeled unhelpfully), meaning that we had to view each one and try to deduce at least minimal information so we could describe the contents. However, the most challenging item was a hard drive, carefully wrapped, with a label reading "The contents of this drive can only be accessed at the original computer from the New York Times. If installed at any other computer, you may damage the contents and you may format (wipe out) the drive." We have no idea quite how to approach this so have simply left it alone as is!

Inability to access content saved on obsolete media or in obsolete programs. Lack of secure, redundant, geographically distributed, and reliable preservation storage systems. Lack of system for managing and providing access to born-digital materials that will allow for restricting some content for a period of time and will also help automate some processes like generating checksums, virus checking, extraction of technical metadata from file headers, etc.

Ingestion of compound/complex objects (i.e., objects made of many types of materials at once). We use Google Spreadsheets to compile metadata and file locations, but a solution like BagIt is likely to be more effective. Presentation of complex objects. Determining how to show a user an object consisting of many disparate parts (e.g., a video with a transcript, screenshots, and an associated web page). This is usually considered a prerequisite to ingestion, since an object is only considered accessible if it can be usefully retrieved. We still address this question on an ad hoc basis. Providing granular security options for all content. The technology required to provide very granular control over rights and permissions makes it difficult to build services for ingesting and reusing repository content. Few repository systems (we use Fedora) have a fully developed solution in this regard, so we use our own solution based on the university's Shibboleth identity system.

Lack of a standard set of best practice guidelines for dealing with original context (e.g., file system hierarchy) of born-digital files when ingesting. Lack of a policy on file format normalization, and identification of what a "record copy" means in the born-digital context. Fear and misunderstanding of the nature of born-digital material.

Lack of software and/or hardware to read files and physical media: We rely on library and college IT departments to access file content, and we acquire legacy hardware when possible. Lack of server space to use for transfer of records from digital media: We recently acquired server space hosted by the university's IT department for use in backing up digital media. Maintaining privacy and security of confidential records; complying with university policy as well as federal and state laws governing privacy: We have policies governing access to confidential records, but procedures specific to born-digital materials are still being developed.

Legacy File Format Normalization: We have a collection that includes over 25 different file extensions, mostly text-based documents, many of which were unrecognized and/or created significant artifacts or "garbage" when rendered in modern programs. A lot of these files were created on the now defunct and unsupported Nota Bene annotation/bibliography software. We used a conversion tool called FileMerlin to convert as many of the troubling files as we could and a Windows Command Line script utilizing Microsoft Word to convert Wordperfect and other Legacy File formats that Word would recognize. After a significant amount of manual and automated work, we increased the number of legible files in the collection from around 40% to around 95%. Legacy Media recovery: Like many institutions, we have many "hybrid" collections that include legacy media such as 3.5"/5 1/4" floppies, hard drives, CD/DVD, even whole computing environments. We are building a Legacy Archival Media Migration Platform (LAMMP) and an accompanying manual as an environment and a workflow for capturing images of these media and generating metadata and capturing contents where possible. We have finished developing and testing this process and are ready to image our first batch of 3.5" floppies, followed shortly by 5 1/4" floppies and hard drive after we acquire the hardware (drives, drivers and write blockers).

Legacy software: needed legacy equipment to access and transfer files. Donated mixed material collections: donor may not own rights to all of collection that was contributed. Images in dissertations that might have fair use rights but not necessarily general dissemination rights: how to deal with this.

Limited staff comfortable with ingest. Although we have an ingest process that has now been formalized and undertaken with more than 50 accessions, we still only have a couple of staff members who possess the sufficient technical skills and understanding of digital records issues to undertake even the rudimentary steps in the accessioning process. This leads to resource constraint issues as more and more digital records on media are being taken in, even if they are not actively collected. To grow this program more, we need more, and lower-level staff to undertake much of the accessioning process, as they currently do with paper. Minimal description practices don't match ingest process. We are following and forensic model of accessions where we are creating forensic images of storage media during accessioning and setting those images aside for further processing. However, the current model for archival accessioning on paper is to undertake minimal arrangement and description during the accessioning process, thereby eliminating a backlog requiring future processing. Hardware and software ingest lab development was time consuming and difficult. Although we have now built up a significant shared lab to enable the ingest of born-digital records from many different types of storage media, the process of building such a lab took several years, expertise, and funding. Each new collection seems to bring new technical issues that must be dealt with.

Major issue is technological — especially how to receive content from private donors. Still being worked on.

Media obsolescence/failure. This includes outmoded storage systems like 5.25" floppy disks and zip disks. Even if we have hardware to accommodate them, we sometimes find that the content is corrupted or otherwise inaccessible. We have a small collection of old drives and other resources nearby; after that we consider outsourcing but will often store as is or even deaccession, depending on resources and anticipated value of the content. Software obsolescence: sometimes it isn't even obsolete, it's just got a small market share, like AskSam. So far, we have been able to find programs to access and migrate/normalize this content. File formats: we have received proprietary camcorder files, for example, which we had difficulty assessing the value of. Upon further investigation, these were found to be metadata files and thumbnails. We determined in the end that we would keep them.

Met with outgoing dean and transferred email account to library servers once he left the position. Outlook PSTs are highly proprietary. Transferred deceased faculty member's email account to library servers. Mac to Windows migration was very time consuming. Email account is Eudora and no easy way to convert emails to less proprietary format. Transferred digitized president's office correspondence from CDs to library servers. Transfer process took hours.

Obsolete file formats. Readability of legacy media. Lack of identifying information accompanying legacy media (unlabeled, no contextual information).

Obsolete media storage. To date we have been able to outsource this to a vendor. Lack of any repository to store or manage personal materials donated. We've taken in a few batches of material and have stored them with only a promise of byte stream recovery and have temporarily turned other material away.

Obsolete media, file systems, and file-formats; e.g. 8" floppy disks, FAT variant disk formats, and WordStar files (existing converters did not work). Data loss from media corruption. Managing the politics surrounding SEI/PII. Some disks have content the donor did not expect to be there, was private, and outside of our collecting scope. Some capture mechanisms are poor or incomplete compared to the original versions; e.g., social media and enterprise systems data.

Obsolete or deteriorating storage media: floppy and optical disks. We are in the process of transferring materials received on such media to networked storage, to facilitate bit-level preservation. Obsolete or unknown file formats. We currently rely on available open-source file identification tools, the file-conversion features of desktop applications, such as MS Word, and the expertise of contract staff familiar with the history of common office work applications. Metadata capture and management. Metadata for born-digital special collections materials is currently managed using the Special Collections databases for accessioning and archival description information. We plan to transition in the near future to a digital repository application with more sophisticated metadata management functionality.

One of the biggest challenges we have faced with our collections is how to satisfactorily handle security and privacy concerns of our donors. Because it is still early days with born-digital personal collections, we are approaching this problem by proposing a process that ensures donor confidence, reviewing outcomes then suggesting other approaches that enable more sustainable practices while also addressing donor concerns. We continue to struggle with identifying archivist-friendly tools to use for ingest and processing. All we can do for now is follow development of tools and best practices in the field. Securing dedicated staffing for digital archives work continues to be a challenge. We now have one dedicated staff member, the promise of another dedicated archivist, and support from other library divisions. Advocacy with senior management about the needs and importance of digital archives has been our only approach.

Opening Legacy formats. Privacy/Security issues of PII. Workflow for ingest.

Organization: Research Data and Institutional Archives come on unorganized file systems. Files need to be restructured into standard, flattened directories representing collections of items. This requires significant analysis and scripting. Metadata: ETDs come from the vendor with transformable metadata. However, metadata is usually non-existent in Research Data and Institutional Archives. Sometimes it can be derived from full text from documents. In the case of audio, video and images, it must be entered or derived from external spreadsheets. Disk Space: Archives are guaranteed preservation only if stored on enterprise data storage. Redundant, highly available enterprise disk is still costly. Traditional administrative systems use relatively small amounts of storage so the infrastructure must ramp up an order of magnitude. An entire integrated library system runs on less than half a terabyte while Research Data collections often utilize 1–10 terabytes each. This creates issues around scheduling and funding disk space acquisition.

Organizations of born-digital material. Have created separate master list that contains organization data. Archiving data as brought in in appropriate format. Standardizing metadata and quality control.

"Preservation environment" vs. "Repository." "Repository" is currently under development. Unwritten vs. written policy (Policy is still under development). "In permanent develop." Most ingest software is in an alpha or beta release, with long-term roadmaps for future development.

Pressure from donors and partner institutions that want us to be able to handle all existing file formats. We're just beginning to grapple with questions of workflow, appraisal, and how to make the files available for research use. Metadata: how much and who creates it? So far we've received a lot of assistance from our technical services unit for materials being ingested in our IR, but we can't expect them to take on that burden for born-digital archival materials, emails, etc.

Privacy: partially addressed through limited access by staff and warnings that material is restricted.

Readability of legacy media: some disks that were accessioned in the past are now unreadable. We currently do not have a strategy to address this. Appraisal: some legacy media acquired in the past was accessioned as part of a larger collection without thought to whether the disk content has sufficient research value to warrant preservation. We now need to decide whether or not to reappraise this material. File format: legacy media has a variety of file formats, many of which are no longer in use. We are piloting the Archivematica preservation system, which will normalize some formats into an access and/or preservation standard.

Redundant storage. Obsolescence. File/data management.

Right now, the libraries do not really have a plan and they are all ingesting born-digital files in different ways. Mostly, materials are kept on external hard drives or in their original legacy media.

Server space: inadequate space for our current digital projects and lack of understanding from administration that there is a need for special collection to have their own serve for processing digital collection. Digital preservation: would like to be part of a LOCKSS system. Currently we are saving our digital collection on main library server as well as the university's server. Next step LOCKSS. Hardware: acquiring legacy computers, working with other departments on campus to identify and locate existing hardware.

Stable storage: large enough; offers growth; limits access. Have just implemented new Isilon mass storage utility. Born-digital mystery files. Purchasing legacy hardware; need forensics software. Workflow to ensure preservation master and deliver use or access copies. With installation of Isilon, parts in place, more discussions underway.

Staffing and time required. Funding. Technology resources.

Staffing: lack of staff positions to address preservation of digital and born-digital content. Challenge addressed in part by re-defining a vacant archivist position as an "e-Archivist" position. We also write additional staff positions into grants wherever feasible (currently we have 4 FTE on grant-funded appointments). Also, existing staff have had new responsibilities added to their job descriptions to support digital preservation efforts. Legacy hardware/software: first tests of born-digital content found in mostly paper archival collections had a low success rate of content acquisition. Challenge will be addressed in part by identification of legacy devices and software by our IT group and in part by our purchase of the "FRED" digital forensics package. We have not yet done a detailed inventory to identify and document types of born-digital content in our collections. Storage: our current archival storage infrastructure was scaled to accommodate our analog to digital digitization program. We projected needing 70TB (replicated 3X) to serve needs through the end of FY2013. Now newer born-digital preservation and access projects will take us far beyond 70TB. Our response has been to begin planning now for a significant increase (to 250TB) at the beginning of FY2013. All funding will be reallocated from existing library budgets.

Storage space: library IT has bought new servers, and the library is collaborating with the campus Center for Advanced Research Computing for additional server space. Permissions (privacy): it will continue to be a challenge to maintain appropriate access and privacy permissions. We are working with various systems (DSpace, CONTENTdm) to explore possibilities of restricting access to specific individuals. Findability: data made available through online servers needs to be findable. We are adding metadata records to our institutional repository that describe datasets available online.

Storage that is secure, backed-up properly with sufficient room for growth. Appropriate workflows to ensure the accurate ingest of born-digital materials. Playback equipment that can extract content safely. Allocation of staff time to focus on issues, develop policy and conduct test pilots to ensure a more proactive process.

Technological support: have to find resources (storage) where we can.

The biggest challenge that our library has faced in obtaining the hardware and software necessary to ingest and manage born-digital materials. We are currently beginning a pilot project using Rosetta and hope that this will enable us to better handle born-digital materials. The second major challenge is the issue of personally identifiable information (PII) in born-digital collections and what to do with it. We currently have no policies for dealing with PII but hope to devise some as part of our Rosetta pilot project. The third major challenge is training our curatorial staff how to deal with born-digital materials--this includes ingesting born-digital materials. We have been working actively with the Conference of Inter-Mountain Archivists to bring several of SAA's Digital Archives Specialist (DAS) courses to our region and are strongly encouraging our curators to participate in these workshops.

These challenges from Presidential Libraries are representative of the challenges other parts of NARA also experience. Volume of data to be ingested in as short a time frame as possible: We receive the vast majority of our electronic records in large transfers at the end of a Presidential administration. Because of our need to provide asset-level access to electronic records as soon as the records are in our legal custody we need to ingest these large volumes in as short a time frame as is possible. In our last large transfer we worked with the records creators and with our system vendor to devise a means of transfer that employed storage area networks (SANs) to move large volumes (tens of terabytes) of data copied from the creator's data center to the data center for our Electronic Records Archives (ERA). Four physical shipments of data stored on SANs over the course of several months moved more than 70TB of data from the source data center to our data center, where the files could be staged for ingest and then moved into our system environment. File-level access control policy: Our system users are located across the country. All users fill the same role in the system, but users should have access to only subsets of the electronic records maintained in the system (Presidential records from one administration versus Vice Presidential records from another administration, for instance). To maintain asset-level access control (among other needs) we established asset catalog entries (ACEs) that were assigned to each asset upon ingest. These ACEs (xml files) include elements that define each asset by a Presidential administration and by a records status (Presidential, Vice Presidential, or Federal). When users log in to Executive Office of the President instance of the Electronic Records Archives (EOP ERA) the system is able to compare the rights of the user to the characteristics of assets to determine if the user can have access to the files. Need to make electronic message files accessible: The storage architecture deployed in EOP ERA makes hundreds of formats available for indexing, including .eml files for emails. One set of electronic messages planned for transfer to us during the last transition (more than 20 million files) was stored in a journal format that maintained the messages as text files. Because we wanted to access the messages as emails (i.e., using parametric searches of email fields – To, From, Date, etc.) our vendor (Lockheed Martin) developed a script that transformed the text files into discrete .eml files that could be ingested into EOP ERA and managed as email files. As part of this transformation process the vendor used sample data to inform a discussion with our archivists on the fields we wanted to maintain in the .eml target files. As part of testing we were able to assure ourselves that the content of the messages came through the transformation intact, including any files attached to the original message files.

There is no Digital Asset Management System (DAMS) in place to ingest born-digital material. System wide initiatives would address this problem. The necessary hardware to transfer born-digital material from legacy media is not available at our repository. A few pieces of legacy hardware have been purchased. Staff expertise to deal with ingesting born-digital materials is limited. This has not yet been addressed.

Time: Reformatting legacy media, and arranging and describing born-digital content, are time-consuming activities. The volume of data that can be found within a single item such as a hard drive can be staggering. Migrating content from legacy media is also time consuming as there is little automation/batch handling of these materials. We are investigating ways in which to reduce time spent on individual items. Migrating unidentified content: With unidentified content on an obsolete media format it's difficult to determine whether the content is a reformatting priority without accessing the material. If we do not have the equipment in-house for the obsolete media format the item requires access by a vendor. Sending an item out to a vendor is expensive and may not be the best use of our resources. At this point, we are investigating ways to address this issue without overuse of resources. Software licensing: Due to stringent state regulations on software purchasing and needing obsolete software titles to access files that may be generations removed from current software (or without a contemporary equivalent) acquiring appropriate software necessary for file migration is a challenge. We are looking into software titles that can bridge generations; that is, software that can open older files and convert them to a newer generation that can be accessed with current software. We are also examining software designed to open obsolete file formats such as Quick View Pro.

Training of existing staff and addition of trained staff to handle the quantity of incoming digital materials expeditiously. Better administrative interface and workflows for staff members ingesting born-digital content. Appraisal of an increasing volume of born-digital materials efficiently.

Unknown file formats. Inadequate software for specialized file formats (e.g., CAD files).

User contributed file formats: some of the content is not is a standard format. Talk to potential donors about contributing content that confirm to open standards. File size: one of the platform that we use is hosted DSpace. If files are too large to upload we work with the vendor to load materials. Restricted items: we try to restrict the materials so that they are available to certain communities.

Variations in file formats, packaging, naming schemes. Applications needed to access content. Lack of clear preservation policies and procedures.

Visible vs. dark archiving. Larger institutional inertia on issue of electronic records management.

Volume of materials, how to appraise. Quality of data, e.g., image files that have low resolution. Not address how to provide access to digital materials when associated with analog collections.

We are managing somewhere between 50,000 and 100,000 digital files on media and server space. We are attempting to copy files from media to server to ensure backup. We have only recently been given permission to load materials to the digital repository, but we have received no additional staff to produce metadata at the item level. We have four pilot projects in progress using paraprofessional staff and interns for metadata production. We want to continue collecting certain basic university publications (i.e., course catalogs) that are formerly paper and now either database driven or web publications. We are negotiating workflows and agreements with producing offices and vendors to produce a continuous online backfile of certain critical titles.

We are working out issues relating to born-digital materials and have not encountered significant challenges with what we have done so far, postponing the more problematic aspects until we get there.

We have born-digital materials on CD and DVD for which there is no server space or metadata provided by the creator of the materials. We address this through a redundant array of external hard drives and back up that is merely a stopgap solution to the problem. We have no expressed authority or access to most born electronic records in other systems such as Banner, so there is no way to review such records for historical value. An ad hoc records advisory committee recently approached Administration requesting creation of an electronic records committee with oversight authority to address these issues campus-wide.

Whether or not the quality of the born-digital is up to par with our institutional benchmarks and guidelines for digital media. In some cases, re-capture is not possible. Discussion with our working group will then include whether a poor copy will be included in the digital library or not. Dealing with file formats that may or may not be compatible (or able to be migrated) with current guidelines of institutional practice. We will test the file to see if a comparable format is acceptable or if data is lost during this process. Sometimes, this will allow our group to explore different presentation tools for other file formats, or we have the option of storing the file only (no automatic presentation tool).

STORAGE POLICIES AND PROCEDURES

14. Please briefly describe who is responsible for each of the following storage activities/functions (e.g., special collections/archives staff, library IT staff, parent organization IT staff, etc.). N=63

Selecting Storage Solutions

A combination of Special Collections/Archives and library IT staff	18	29%
Library IT staff	14	22%
A combination of library IT and campus IT staff	6	10%
Campus IT staff	3	5%
A combination of Special Collections/Archives, library IT, and campus IT staff	3	5%
Other	19	30%

Ad hoc committees led by central library IT

Archives, digital curation leadership, and library network/system administration

Digital Services and Shared Collections Department and Digital Development and Web Services Unit, in conjunction with institution-wide IT

Digital Strategies committee (drawing from library IT, Special Collections, and other units within library)

Electronic Records Archives Program Management Office (within Information Services) and Preservation Staff (within Research Services)

For the repository, the Director of Integrated Information Systems works with a team, including network administrators and the digital data curator. The Special Collections/University Archives staff will lead a library (possibly university) team to select an electronic records management system for the university.

Institutional records: a team consisting of the records manager, college archivist, archives staff and institutional IT. Personal materials: college archivist, special collections technology coordinator, manuscripts supervisor.

IT staff at the Southwest Collections/Special Collections Library, Digi Resources Library Unit, and the University Library

Library & parent IT staff/consortia

Library administration (once Library Systems recommends)

Library Information Technology Office and Library Digital Programs Division

Library IT and the Carolina Digital Repository

Library IT and the Office of the CIO

Library IT staff, in consultation with Special Collections and Preservation/Digital Initiatives

Library IT/Digital Initiatives

San Diego Supercomputer Center (SDSC)

Selecting the technology for the institution is handled by our IT Department. Selecting the appropriate tools from the libraries available resources is handled by the curatorial and program management staff.

University Libraries Central Operations department, Digital Preservation Strategist

We have a Technical Architecture Council that works in concert with collection managers and IT staff to select.

Implementing and Maintaining Storage Infrastructure

Library IT staff	28	44%
A combination of library IT and campus IT staff	14	22%
A combination of Special Collections/Archives and library IT staff	5	8%
Campus IT staff	4	6%
A combination of Special Collections/Archives, library IT, and campus IT staff	1	2%
Other	11	18%

Archives, digital curation leadership, and library network/system administration

Central Operations department, Digital Preservation Strategist

Digital Services and Shared Collections Department and Digital Development and Web Services Unit, in conjunction with institution-wide IT

Electronic Records Archives Program Management Office (within Information Services) and Preservation Staff (within Research Services)

Institutional records: a team consisting of the records manager, college archivist, archives staff, and institutional IT. Personal materials: library IT.

IT and Scholarly Publishing and Data Management Team

IT staff at the Southwest Collections/Special Collections Library, Digi Resources Library Unit, and the University Library

Library IT and the Office of the CIO

Library IT staff, campus IT, California Digital Library Staff

San Diego Supercomputer Center (SDSC)

Special collections and preservation librarian

Managing Permissions/User Authentication.

Library IT staff	20	32%
A combination of library IT and campus IT staff	8	13%
A combination of Special Collections/Archives and library IT staff	6	10%
Special Collections/Archives staff	3	5%
Campus IT staff	2	3%
A combination of Special Collections/Archives, library IT, and campus IT staff	2	3%
Other	22	35%

A combination of special collections, library administration, library IT, and parent organization IT

Archival Staff \ Digital Initiatives Librarian

Campus/library network/system administration

Central Operations department

Digital Initiatives/collecting unit

Digital Services and Shared Collections Department and Digital Development and Web Services Unit, and Special and Area Studies Collections for permissions to physical materials as they are transferred to digital.

Electronic Records Archives Program Management Office (within Information Services) and Preservation Staff (within Research Services)

Implemented by Libraries IT staff; those with access to secure archival space must be designated by the director of a given unit or her designee.

Institutional records: institutional IT. Personal materials: library IT.

IT staff at the Southwest Collections/Special Collections Library Digi Resources Library Unit and the University Library

Libraries IT staff, Digital Archivist

Library & parent IT staff/consortia

Library Information Technology Office and Library Digital Programs Division

Library IT with input from collection staff

Library IT, curators, and the Office of the CIO

Library Research & learning support unit (where the institutional repository librarian is located)

Non IT digital repository managers and IT

Permissions: Library IT staff. User authentication: Campus IT staff.

San Diego Supercomputer Center (SDSC)

Shared responsibility between the IT Department and the system owners. May also be based on license or other agreements governing our content.

The library works with the Office of Information Technology to use LDAP, CAS and Shibboleth IdM for single sign on, but may also implement authentication microservices for specific projects. These are designed by the digital library architects and implemented by digital library programmers.

We're still working through these issues. We use the campus LDAP for our institutional repository. Other instances are managed by library IT and/or Digital Initiatives librarians.

Estimating Storage Needs

A combination of Special Collections/Archives and library IT staff	16	25%
Special Collections/Archives staff	11	18%
Library IT staff	9	14%
A combination of library IT and campus IT staff	1	2%
Campus IT staff	0	—
A combination of Special Collections/Archives, library IT, and campus IT staff	0	—
Other	26	41%

Archival Staff/ Digital Initiatives Librarian

Archives, digital curation leadership and library network/system administration

Central Operations department, Digital Library Services department

Collection staff

Digital Archivist, Libraries IT staff

Digital Collection Managers

Digital Initiative Librarians, Data Curation Librarians, Library IT

Digital Initiatives/Library IT

Digital Services and Shared Collections Department and Digital Development and Web Services Unit

Directors, Library/Archives staff, IT staff

Each collector/selector

Electronic Records Archives Program Management Office (within Information Services)

Institutional records: a team consisting of the records manager, college archivist, archives staff and institutional IT. Personal materials: library IT.

IT Department, based on input from the curatorial and program management staff.

IT staff at the Southwest Collections/Special Collections Library Digi Resources Library Unit and the University Library

Library & parent IT staff/consortia

Library Digital Programs Division

Library IT and curators

Library IT staff with Library Research & learning support unit

Library IT staff/collection curators/reformatted content producers (e.g., those migrating content from obsolete media into a modern format.)

Library Systems with input from Digital Library Services and Special Collections & University Archives

Research Data Curation staff

Special Collections to project what and how collections will grow, library IT to project what resources are needed and cost.

Special collections/archives staff, digital collections staff, library IT

Special Collections/preservation librarian

The Director of Integrated Information Systems and the Digital Data Curator

Budgeting Storage Usage

Library IT staff	22	36%
A combination of Special Collections/Archives and library IT staff	11	18%
A combination of library IT and campus IT staff	3	5%
Special Collections/Archives staff	2	3%
Campus IT staff	0	—
A combination of Special Collections/Archives, library IT, and campus IT staff	0	—
Other	22	36%

Administration

Archives, digital curation leadership and library network/system administration

Budgeting storage usage is determined at this time by Library Administration, Library IT staff, and Special Collections and Archives staff.

Central Operations department

Currently, the libraries are not allocating storage usage by project except in cases where grant funding has purchased specific storage amounts.

Digital collections

Digital Initiatives Librarians, Library IT

Digital Initiatives/Library IT

Digital Services and Shared Collections Department and Digital Development and Web Services Unit, in conjunction with Fiscal Services

Directors, Library/Archives staff, IT Staff

Electronic Records Archives Program Management Office (within Information Services) and Preservation Staff (within Research Services)

Head of Systems and Director of Administrative Services

Institutional records: a team consisting of the records manager, college archivist, archives staff and institutional IT. Personal materials: library IT.

Libraries IT staff, Digital Archivist

Library Administration, Library IT staff

Library Information Technology Office and Library Digital Programs Division

Library IT and curators

Library Technology Council (represents all stakeholders for technology issues)

N/A; based on pay for use.

Parent IT staff/consortia

Research Data Curation staff

Southwest Collections Administration and Library Technology Management System

Monitoring Storage Usage

Library IT staff	25	40%
A combination of Special Collections/Archives and library IT staff	10	16%
A combination of library IT and campus IT staff	5	8%
Special Collections/Archives staff	2	3%
Campus IT staff	0	—
A combination of Special Collections/Archives, library IT, and campus IT staff	0	—
Other	18	29%

Central Operations department

Digital Archivist, Libraries IT staff

Digital collections

Digital Initiatives Librarians, Library IT

Digital Initiatives/Library IT

Digital Services and Shared Collections Department and Digital Development and Web Services Unit

Electronic Records Archives Program Management Office (within Information Services) and Preservation Staff (within Research Services)

Institutional records: institutional IT. Personal materials: library IT.

IT staff at the Southwest Collections/Special Collections Library, Digi Resources Library Unit and the University Library

Library Digital Programs Division

Library IT staff monitor and advise Special Collections and Archives staff regarding storage.

Library IT staff with Library Research & learning support unit

Library Systems, Digital Library Services, Special Collections & University Archives

Not currently undertaken.

Parent IT staff/consortia

Research Data Curation staff

Special Collections/preservation librarian

The Director of Integrated Information Systems and the Digital Data Curator

Budgeting Storage Funding

Library administration	14	22%
Library IT staff	14	22%
A combination of Special Collections/Archives and library IT staff	6	10%
Special Collections/Archives staff	3	5%
A combination of library administration and library IT staff	2	3%
A combination of library IT and campus IT staff	2	3%
A combination of library administration, Special Collections/Archives, and library IT	2	3%
A combination of library administration and campus IT staff	1	2%
Other	18	29%

Associate University Librarian for Digital Library Systems

Central Operations department

Digital Initiatives/Library IT

Digital Services and Shared Collections Department and Digital Development and Web Services Unit, in conjunction with Fiscal Services

Digital Strategies Committee

Directors

Each collector/selector is responsible, although few actually undertake this task.

Head of Systems and Director of Administrative Services

Institutional records: institutional IT. Personal materials: library IT.

IT staff and Scholarly Publishing and Data Management Team

Library Information Technology Office and Libraries Administrative Services

Library IT staff, and Associate University Librarian for Digital & Discovery Services

Electronic Records Archives Program Management Office (within Information Services)

Parent IT staff/consortia

Requested an annual basis—IT and library staff.

Research Data Curation staff

Shared by library departments.

Southwest Collections Administration and Library Technology Management System

Other Storage Activity/Function

Arts Library work stored on local HD or external HD until pushed to I&D.

Digital preservation activities are carried out by special collections/archives staff working with Libraries IT.

Planning storage architecture: Library IT with Carolina Digital Repository

Special Collections and Archives are responsible for managing physical storage of legacy media containing born electronic materials.

Tape storage: Archives staff

We have a couple of strategies for ensuring files that are persistent and authentic, including multiple online, nearline, and offline copies and regular signature verification for each preserved file.

15. Please indicate which of the following storage solutions your library uses for ingest, processing, access, back up, and long-term "dark" storage. Check all that apply. N=63

	Ingest	Processing	Access	Back up	Storage	N
External Media Library (e.g., CD/DVDs, tapes, loose drives)	41	18	27	31	16	59
IT-supported Network File System	35	43	43	44	26	58
Local/Attached storage (e.g., internal drive, external drive or other local storage device)	46	43	27	23	14	57
Distributed computing/storage systems (e.g., LOCKSS or iRods)	4	4	6	16	19	21
Cloud storage (e.g., DuraCloud, Amazon S3, Google Storage, Mozy, or Box.net)	5	2	6	4	4	12
Other solution	7	5	10	6	8	15
Number of Responses	61	57	60	58	50	63

If you selected "Other Solution" above, please briefly describe the solution below.

Other solution for ingest N=7

Bagit transfer protocol.

Cloud storage is currently used on a limited basis for ingest; we plan to investigate its use for the other categories listed in this survey.

Consortium provides web-based ingestion, processing, and access for thesis and dissertations.

Currently all are being reviewed.

Hosted Open Repository.

Library IT runs a collection development instance of DSpace on its own server.

OnBase.

Other solution for processing N=4

Consortium provides web-based ingestion, processing, and access for thesis and dissertations.

Currently all are being reviewed.

Library IT runs a collection development instance of DSpace on its own server.

OnBase.

Other solution for access N=9

Amazon Cloud, hosted Open Repository.

Consortium provides web-based ingestion, processing, and access for thesis and dissertations.

Currently, all are being reviewed.

Local implementation of a Fedora repository.

Shared servers with IT on campus.

Local DSpace instance; California Digital Library's Web Archiving Service; system-wide open access repository.

We are still working this out.

We use OhioLINK for some digital content, not necessarily born-digital content.

YouSendIt & email have both been used to provide access to materials.

Other solution for back up N=5

Amazon Cloud, hosted Open Repository.

California Digital Library's Merritt Repository (content repository, geographically separate).

Currently, all are being reviewed.

Redundant storage managed by campus and library IT.

Virtual and physical tape storage

Other solution for long-term, dark storage N=7

California Digital Library's Merritt Repository (content repository, geographically separate).

Chronopolis.

Currently all are being reviewed.

Isilon.

Redundant storage managed by campus and library IT.

Virtual and physical tape storage.

We do not have "dark storage" per se. Instead we use Fedora as an asset management system where "master files" (e.g., tiffs) are copied to our replicated storage systems for long-term preservation, with appropriate preservation metadata and restricted access.

16. Please briefly describe how your library estimates future digital storage needs and costs. N=44

Analyze past usage and extrapolate future as well as monitoring use on a monthly basis.

Archives use virtual servers for digital storage, and adds storage as needed. Pays monthly fee to central IT. Estimate 5TB year. Libraries use a combination of local storage area network, remote storage area network, and offline tape backup. Estimates are based on current collection growth and future predictions for growth. Currently operate with 30TB headroom for approximately 30TB of data.

Assessing past growth rates, adjusting for known projects forthcoming in the next year. Estimates are also adjusted to incorporate the storage needs related to grant-funded projects. At this point, costs are estimated based on current costs for disks, storage devices, and backups. We are, however, looking at ways of moving to endowment-based models for some of our storage costs.

Based on current usage and growth over time. We currently have over 15TB online and 100TB in dark archive storage and have reports for growth over time.

Based on growth rates for past digital collections projects.

Based on projecting growth from current collections and rate of estimated future reformatting and ingest.

Can't answer, this is done by library IT.

Collection staff are polled regularly and asked for estimates of incoming born-digital materials.

Curatorial and project management staff submit estimates on a quarterly basis. The IT department then analyzes the needs and costs for budgeting and acquisition purposes.

Curators consult with our digital preservation officer and estimate possible future digital storage needs based on past needs.

Currently done by IT library staff. Anticipating using L.I.F.E. model for anticipating curation/lifecycle costs. Processing storage vs. long-term archival storage.

Digital Library Services staff provide yearly estimates on the growth of digital assets in the system. Estimated growth is determined through an evaluation of existing programmatic support as well as identifying particular projects that may bring in additional assets. A longitudinal analysis is also done to see how we are trending over time in terms of our digital storage growth. This information is presented to Central Operations staff for use in budgeting and storage acquisition decisions.

Estimate based on storage growth in previous years.

Extrapolating from current use and engaging with vendors/partners (i.e., CDL).

Future digital storage needs will be scaled to the development of campus department operations. The trick is to develop a system that is flexible, sustainable, and migratable.

Future storage needs and costs are managed through the ERA Program Management Office, who must balance the storage needs of all the instances of ERA against the most cost-effective storage approaches.

Have not yet.

Libraries IT solicits estimates from special collections/archives for the next year's usage and needs. Estimates are based on past usage and growth and anticipated projects. Anticipated projects may be either digitization projects or born-digital content we expect to receive.

Moved away from DVDs and external drivers (except occasionally for ingest) and work directly on server (IT supported Network File System) for all steps in the process. Storage needs: so far, have depended on the recommendations from DLI programmers and systems staff.

Needs are estimated based on known incoming materials in the short term, ideally several weeks/months in advance. We will gradually add TB of storage space as needed.

Not applicable at this time. Pending.

Our storage projections account for our born-digital and locally digitized materials and are based on the fact that we will have a number of file types which, both in their native and any normalized formats, are quite large: for example, uncompressed tiff files and video files, and large datasets. Costs are determined by library and central IT.

Our units look at recent activity requiring digital storage, and at future projects and goals to estimate our upcoming storage needs.

Past years' growth and projected new acquisitions of born-digital collections.

Planned digitization activities or acquisitions of born-digital material are planned for the fiscal year. Storage amounts required to accommodate that digital content are devised based on average file size for a particular type of record. Costs for this storage are estimated based on current market value, usually at the TB level.

Planning for digital storage needs and costs is the responsibility of the library systems department and the Associate University Librarian, Digital & Discovery Services, with consultations with department heads on their storage needs for ongoing activities and special projects.

Project by project, case by case.

Read research and follow trends. (Our recent move to Cloud storage for example. Once method is tested by other institutions and proven to be trust-worthy.)

Still developing.

The Digital Data Curator and Director of IIS monitor storage utilization and recommend purchases for grants and for annual purchase based on the types of materials currently stored and anticipated storage needs for project in planning or currently under way.

The library is working on a plan to estimate future storage needs now. Currently it is just allocated on an as-needed basis.

The recent inventory is a first step. In addition to the inventory curators have been asked to estimate growth rates. Library IT is investigating storage options including the cloud and cost models for storage.

This is a process receiving on-going development. Currently, space needs are estimated given past collecting volume + a 20% inflator and any known collections we anticipate receiving. Costs are estimated by the library IT staff based on the cost for the storage they lease from the university's Office of Information Technology.

Track historical usage and growth contrasting the resultant data with projections/requests previously provided from librarians. This provides a delta of growth not contained in a long-term plan. Track usage from new initiatives. Categorize the data by type; identifying growth areas. An example of historical usage follows: in November of 1999, the fileserver had 5 GB of disk storage available for all library employees. In 2000, there was approximately 30 GB of storage made available. In April of last year we were backing up around 10 TB of data. Currently we back up 18 TB of data. This data is "information" versus server images, etc. An example of a new initiative: The Dean has expressed a strong desire to have all data replicated and online off-site which would bring the immediate potential usage to 36 TB. This amount has to be doubled due to redundancy on our ISCSI SAN (72TB) and multiplied by 1.17 to factor in RAID (84 TB). Plus, keep a 24TB node on site for redundancy (108TB). Since technology changes, we always start with the original amount of "real" data. Rule of thumb, consumption generally increases by a factor of 2 to 4 within a 12–18 month period. However, create a new department, get a grant, etc. and projections and planning is not quite worthless, but….. Prepare short term solutions for immediate growth needs (generally encountered through some event horizon effect). If a list of digital collections and their respective size estimates for the next 5 years were to be provided, more precise projections can be made- if no deviations to the plan are allowed. Baring that, any additional new (unexpected) collections should include monies for the growth in disk storage and allow for the delivery of the necessary hardware.

University IT storage fees plus staff time.

We are in the process of assessing storage needs for digital archives and University Archives over the next three to five years. We are basing numbers on collection growth expectations and assumptions about the types of media we will likely acquire. Costing models are established by University IT.

We do not currently have a metric for this process, but will be working to develop one.

We don't currently do this. Some staff understand that this is a problem, but few at the executive decision-making levels.

We estimate storage needs and costs based on past growth and known new projects and commitments. We also add estimates for possible and unpredictable needs insofar as possible. We do careful hardware and market analysis to determine best vendors, configurations, and prices.

We have a pipeline of projects, estimate space per project and negotiate with Central IT for space. The library's DSpace server acts as a buffer until production, enterprise space becomes available.

We have built an Excel spreadsheet that lists expected and 'prospected' collections and collaborative projects and their estimated storage amounts; and used formulas based on cost of Isilon, support, and staffing, for example: 10 hours/ video = 1TB = $3000/5 years of storage on Isilon.

We plan on using DuraCloud and Peachnet (cloud storage) for future external storage and replication. Estimates are based on current storage needs with estimated growth rate of 4TB per year.

We project ingestion of electronic records residing on legacy media in the future, but have no way of accurately estimating born electronic records residing in systems like Banner.

We're still working on the best way to estimate future needs. Currently, frequent communication about upcoming projects helps estimate these needs.

17. Please briefly describe up to three challenge(s) your library has faced in storing born-digital materials (e.g., amount of storage, security/ability to store sensitive data, ease of access to digital materials in long-term storage, cost, technical skills in setting up and managing storage, etc.) and how the library has addressed that challenge. N=57

Storage Challenges Word Cloud

Ability to store various kinds of data, ease of access to materials in long-term storage. We are working with an external consultant to establish digital preservation services, including long-term storage.

Accessibility of electronic records: Because of our need to search and access a heterogeneous body of electronic records at the individual asset level we needed a storage solution that supported indexing and searching for an array of formats. EOP ERA uses the Hitachi Content Platform storage architecture, which indexes hundreds of file formats, including the email and various office automation products that comprise the majority of the records in our holdings. Our deployment of the Hitachi platform includes the FAST search engine, which allowed us to develop search interfaces that correspond to the predominant types of records in our collections. Balancing ease of access with security. The amount of storage necessary to ingest and reserve federal agency records and the cost for the massive amount of storage that will be needed over the long haul.

Acquiring adequate volume of storage at a reasonable cost. Our A/V collections consume a large amount of space and all our materials require security and redundancy. Tiered storage solutions would provide more cost-effective solutions, however they are not available to us. We have materials in several locations and we do not have adequate means of tracking what materials are stored where. The coordination to increase network security around sensitive dark storage has been difficult. Miscommunication across four different groups for this new service has been a very slow process.

Administrative reorganization: Libraries is reliant on the university's IT department (IST) to purchase and set up digital storage. IST is undergoing a major reorganization making it very difficult for staff to be assigned to carry out the Libraries' requests for storage. A new CIO has been hired to finalize the reorganization process. Libraries has investigated cloud storage as an alternative to IST. Size of digital files: the Archives has acquired several TBs of born-digital records and has created several more through its ongoing digitization efforts. This fact, in combination with IST's difficulty in enabling additional storage, results in the Archives quickly exhausting existing storage options.

Centralization: our situation will likely be exacerbated by the fact that the Libraries' IT staff will soon be subsumed by the university's IT staff in its efforts to centralize functions. We can expect greater delays in acquiring and managing digital storage when we lose our dedicated IT staff who were previously responsible for these tasks.

All is in flux and subject to change, but we are developing a DAMS and staffing to develop that system is slender. We have one programmer on the job, making progress. Need to address security/privacy issues more fully than we have and develop comprehensive (rather than case by case) strategies.

Amount of storage: continually asking for more. Explaining how this is different than a preservation repository, which the materials will go into but until they are processed. Ensuring stability of the files.

Amount of storage: current university infrastructure does not have capacity for a large amount of born-digital material. Future upgrades should take in to account an exponential increase in expected storage need. Secure access: For those items we choose not to or cannot store on campus, choosing a cloud-based solution is difficult because of PATRIOT Act issues. This is an ongoing issue. Staff expertise: IT staff are not necessarily versed in maintaining archival quality records. This is primarily a staff training issue, not a technological one.

Amount of storage: We nearly ran out of space this year due to the way the servers were configured and allocated. The problem was that a server had been called into service to temporarily house a system from a failing server. This issue was temporary, as the system is being migrated to a new server, but it is indicative of space budgeting problems. We have not always been accurate in our predictions of space needs. We have recently moved to a VMware solution that should help by providing greater flexibility. Cost: This has historically been a problem. Initially, collecting areas that took in or created digital content were expected to pay for their own servers, but in recent years this has become an accepted part of the Libraries IT department's responsibilities. Our costs have also gone down as a result of a move to VMware. Technical skills: most recently this has been in the area of awareness of the need for (and skill in integrating) things like integrity checking and monitoring systems in general. This will be the next step in special collections/archives' collaboration with Libraries IT staff.

Amount of storage has previously been a challenge, but has become less of a problem with the fall in storage costs in recent years. Future storage needs for large-scale ingest of born-digital special collections materials will probably be integrated into university-wide planning for digital repositories, a digital asset management system, and networked storage & continuity planning. Technical skills of special collections staff in managing born-digital materials has been a challenge, which was initially solved by contract staff with the required skills, and now by hiring a Digital Special Collections Librarian as permanent staff with the required skills. Providing access to born-digital special collections is an ongoing problem, with no unified solution. ETDs are available through a DSpace instance; the university web-archive is hosted externally, with Archive-It. Copies of other born-digital materials in special collections or university archives fonds are usually provided to researchers on a cost-recovery basis, using optical disks. Future development of a library digital repository will greatly facilitate access to the latter materials.

Amount of storage needed and "non archive" approach of central university IT unit. Still under discussion.

Amount of storage required and costs of storage. Staff resources and funding for managing born-digital records. Time resources for those with technical skills for storage management.

Amount of storage required. Cost.

Amount of storage: working with library IT to provide server space.

Amount of storage; starting to manage temporary alternative file management systems. Ease of access; challenges of ongoing equipment management. Technical skills commitment from institution.

Amount of storage: We have purchased additional disk space. File type/migration: We are in the process of creating a digital preservation policy to limit file types we will manage/migrate. Security: We have developed project teams with limited levels of access, depending on need.

Cost. Distributed storage sites. Long-term storage and access.

Dark archives storage is less of a preservation environment than the platform for access copies. Storage issues are further exacerbated by a lack of central IT understanding of digital preservation requirements. The previously mentioned inventory is the start in a process to get a better handle on storage capacity and digital preservation tool needs. Further, the Libraries have identified the need to develop a digital preservation policy/plan. Staff time and skills to actively ingest, process, and manage born-digital objects. The creation of the e-records/digital resources archivist position is one step in the process. Additionally, curators and curatorial staff are seeking appropriate training opportunities.

Data loss: Moved toward more stable hardware and regularized review. Technical skills: Hiring consultants as well as using combination of library and parent IT.

Disconnect between archival masters, metadata, and access derivatives. Previously these have been in separate systems or in a simple file system. We are implementing a Fedora-based repository service to centralize storage and management of ALL digital materials. Managing rights and access to restricted content. We are working with university IT to implement Shibboleth identity management as one approach to solve this problem. Determining the long-term cost of storing digital content in perpetuity. We are examining pay-once-store-forever vs. subscription management models.

Funding and skills to manage a true digital archive. Amount of storage required.

Having enough storage so that we don't run out during a project. Getting an appropriate system in place for off-site, secure back up. Cost of storage.

High cost of preservation storage infrastructure. This has been addressed for the present by reallocating funds from other parts of the Libraries budget to purchase storage. When feasible we add a one-time storage fee to grant-supported projects. Bandwidth costs. Because of bandwidth costs, we have selected remote storage options that are available via subsidized carriers like NYSERNET or Internet2. These storage options are not necessarily the most cost-effective, however. Changing storage technologies, manufacturer, and vendor churn. We have approached the problem of vendor churn and changing technologies by assuming a rolling five-year model for hardware replacement, assuming that we may have to keep changing vendors and equipment.

I have been delaying moving digital video from media to server space because of the massive file sizes. We also have issues ripping video from certain access formats. I am still requesting MPEG-2 for film/video preservation since it is compressed; don't have time to evaluate sustainability of other formats that might enable increased quality.

In terms of personal materials we have had issues related to ease of access and managing storage. But all of these are potential issues since our current system for personal materials is sketchy.

Insufficient staffing. We continue to explore options within the context of library-wide staffing issues. Long-term storage and access. We continue to work with library IT and university IT. The actual amount of storage needed. We continue to work with library IT and university IT.

Justifying the need for and the resources required for storing multiple copies of large original/master files, in multiple locations, and preserved on an ongoing basis. Affordable, geographically distributed storage. We are evaluating options to distribute storage of our digital materials, mitigating the risks associated with a single location for storage. Costs of large-scale storage. We are reexamining our business models for the storage of digital collections and investigating partnerships that will make it easier for us to manage storage.

Lack dark archive storage structure and toolset. Technical skills to manage stored content appropriately (are currently working with Fedora and associated management tools). Space: cost of long-term storage, especially for content from researchers.

Lack of preservation-quality digital repository. The library has designed and implemented a Fedora-based repository system to serve as a dark archive. Inexperience managing digital files on a server (setting up file structure, etc.) We will collaborate with other library groups to establish consistent best practices. Safe handling of donated servers. We are investigating best practices for handling these materials.

Larger institutional inertia on electronic records management has not yet been addressed. Lack of "one size fits all" solution lowers curatorial enthusiasm for managing born-digital records. Technical solutions/skills/infrastructure also hasn't been addressed yet.

Learning what level and type of metadata must be preserved to accompany the growing amount of born-digital assets, including: adequate Dublin Core records for collections in DSpace; embedded digital metadata; workflow and seeking ways to efficiently transfer existing metadata; how to address concerns about linking to resources and the possible transient nature of links. Selecting versions of materials to be preserved. For example, should files be saved as originally named as received and in the form re-named for local use? Should all formats of images be saved — tiffs, and any derivatives; or wav files and derivatives, or only uncompressed formats? In a way the question is whether we are storing for preservation or to provide an inventory of formats for delivery and service. Archives are guaranteed preservation only if stored on enterprise data storage. Redundant, highly available enterprise disk is still costly.

Long-term storage, backup & mirroring, geographic distribution of mirrored sites: Libraries has worked to include infrastructure expenditure into operating costs. Availability, access restrictions, copyright: library has met these challenges on an ad-hoc basis.

Network Bottlenecks: Moving large amounts of data across our network has been challenging due to bottlenecks which result in failed process and excessive transfer times. This is an issue that we are currently assessing. Storage Capacity: Our present storage capacity has not kept up with the rate of acquiring and generating born-digital materials. Our institution is presently developing a preservation repository that will have increased storage for items that we are interested in keeping in perpetuity. Procuring storage is also difficult. A number of library stakeholders with an interest in digital content will be working on a committee with a member of library IT to address workflow issues that may improve storage efficiency. Security: We are encountering challenges with providing access to materials that are subject to copyright. Although we are reformatting items as deemed acceptable under Section 108 we still have to protect these items from illegal duplication. Thus far, it has been difficult to provide access to these items.

No integrated digital acquisitions plan; planning tends to be on a project basis rather than an overall program. Capacity challenges within our physical technical infrastructure. Ability to manage access based on a wide and changing variety of licensing and access restrictions.

Not enough available server space for storage. A larger server has been purchased. Lack of staff expertise regarding born-digital material storage. This has not yet been addressed.

Our biggest challenge right now is in storage capacity, given the fact that we resort to an array of external hard drives. We are developing a pilot Digital Asset Management System that would expand our capacity. Second would be the need for developing and implementing metadata to effectively address records retention schedules. Long-term storage is the final challenge. Our plan is to develop an effective DAM system with an archival system to ensure preservation and access.

Our biggest challenge with storage continues to be establishing policies and infrastructure that will allow us to integrate born-digital collections into our larger repository infrastructure. Security, complexity of ingested items, and size of objects have been impediments. We are taking a phased approach to ingest and working with our systems staff to address these challenges.

Our storage is currently for archival resources only. Research faculty would really like storage where they can build research data, by continuing to add and revise data until it is ready for permanent ingest. We are currently looking at strategies to segment our space and provide work area utilities. We currently have 47 TB of data storage, which would not be adequate for very large data projects. We do not have a successful working model for assessing the cost of data storage, which we believe needs to be a one-time cost but must provide at least partial cost recovery for managing data over the long term. Most models we have seen are based on the cost of storage, not the cost of staffing for storage, which should include the cost of preparing and describing data.

Quantity of storage available, including appropriate backups. Cost of increasing amounts of storage. Setting up, monitoring, and managing increasing amounts of storage.

Security of sensitive material. We are investigating the ability of Rosetta to segregate materials and allow access by user password. Access to born-digital materials by patrons. We are trying to determine if we need to have a public access system and a dark archive or if one system can do both. This is contingent on solving Challenge 1. Funding storage costs. We are working with the university administration to see if they will fund some storage costs and we are investigating a model where we would grant campus departments a certain amount of space and if they need more, they would pay for it.

Security/ ability to store and manage sensitive data (work in progress). Policies to address storage requirements (work in progress).

Sensitive Data: No Research Data has yet been made public. Access is restricted to the research teams. Our Graduate School has also declined open access to ETDs. Repository ETDs are restricted to staff, but the public can access some through ProQuest.

Server space and the management of that space is a challenge. We have set regular meetings between staff in the unit using the largest amount of storage space and the library IT staff to be sure all are informed on upcoming storage needs.

Storage space and estimating storage space. Coordinating storage. Fixity.

Storage space that is not an external hard drive in someone's office. Still trying to figure out how to handle this. Cost: which system is the most economical but also does what we need it to do. Still trying to figure this out. Access to born-digital materials. Not sure yet.

Storage space. Library IT purchased new servers and is collaborating with campus IT for additional storage space. Restricting permissions to specific viewers is challenging on an administrative level. Digital Initiatives and Data Curation Librarians work with data providers to determine who should have access to data.

Technical requirements in setting up a sustainable digital preservation environment. The Libraries is continuing to define all the aspects that make up a fully functioning preservation environment, looking at the needed policies and procedures, application support and technical infrastructure. Any final policy or plan must fit within and be driven by existing Libraries collecting policies. Issues related to long-term sustainability of assets in a multitude of formats, some standardized and others of a more non-traditional or uniquely proprietary nature. The Libraries is looking to push out support for those submitting files for inclusion in its systems with recommendations for file format types that are more easily sustained or that have proven better for support.

The main challenge is that our existing data that we use to inform storage needs are based on the creation of image collections. Born-digital materials have the potential to be exponentially larger in terms of storage requirements. Distributed storage environments. We have not yet identified a sustainable way to hook our repository services up to other campus storage environments for the purpose of linking and ingestion. Estimating the costs to maintain storage for the long term, including curation and migration costs.

The most significant challenge for storage is the same as one of the challenges for ingest: the lack of an infrastructure of repositories and tools to store and maintain these kinds of materials. While many parts of the process can be handled by established tools, other parts can't or systems don't work together. So, as an example, while we have preservation storage for digital masters of digitized images that can also be used for storage of born-digital materials, this is dark storage and it doesn't meet the need for access and discovery of materials. Similarly, the repository for access and discovery has been designed so far for individual images, e-books, and A/V, not for heterogeneous groups of materials in a manuscript collection that may be described only at an aggregate level in a finding aid. The only way to address this challenge is to develop the infrastructure further and adopt and adapt emerging tools for parts of this process. Related to this is coordination of resources to address these needs. While we, like everyone else, can always use more staff and more funding, just utilizing the staff that we have to address these needs while continuing to address existing needs is a concern. In addition, the infrastructure and workflows created to address these materials cannot exist in a vacuum, they must be compatible with or must be an extension of the infrastructure that manages data about the rest of the library's collections. This means that progress on developing infrastructure in support of born-digital materials must include input, buy-in, and resources from many parts of the library organization: special collections, library IT, administration, technical services, etc. Increasing meaningful communication between groups and jointly planning development is the best way to address these challenges. Another challenge for storage is determining what to store and what metadata to store about it. While a default option is to store a bit-level copy for long-term preservation, some work has been done to determine what other levels of preservation can be supported and what data would need to be stored in order to enable this level of preservation. A significant challenge relates to the retention of private or sensitive information. Given the nature of the archival workflow, we really do not have time to completely process materials before we put them in archival storage. This means that private or sensitive information may be inadvertently stored for some time. We do have some tools we can use during accessioning to automatically search for significant patterns such as SSNs and social security numbers within textual data, but we do not have the time to do any more in-depth searching. While this mirrors the situation with paper records (although, we can actually remove more potentially private information during accessioning with born-digital textual materials than with paper), the risk is much greater for loss of security of this information in the digital environment. An additional issue that we are still considering is how to (or, indeed, whether to) securely dispose of media carriers (disks) that continue to store sensitive data even after a copy has been retrieved from them. The issues are that, in some cases the media carrier itself may retain artifactual value (hand-written annotations, modifications, metadata contained on labels, etc.), if the copy made was corrupt or lost the media can serve as a back-up, and that completely wiping hardware is difficult to do. The recommended options for destruction and deletion of the data are potentially costly and time-consuming (disk shredding, magnetic wiping). To address these challenges we have undertaken a number of activities and are still discussing other solutions. One major step was consulting the library's legal counsel for advice on adhering to university, state, and federal regulations in the handling and storage of this data. Other workflow issues, such as the screening of content for sensitive information at the accessioning stage using automated methods, have also been added to the workflow.

UCISpace Fixity: until recently the material ingested into UCISpace (local DSpace instance) was not being continually checked for fixity/authenticity. We now run a checksum checker on all UCISpace content nightly and are in the final stages of implementing a system that will back up DSpace generated AIPs of all UCISpace material into CDL's Merritt repository. This Merritt collection will serve as a geographically separate dark archive that we can also access to replace lost or corrupted items/collections if and when the checksum checker discovers them. Canto Cumulus: a robust digital asset management system that our Special Collections and Archives department uses for managing media collections, mostly digitized and born-digital images. However, it has a steep learning curve and is not very user friendly, and we have had difficulty obtaining vendor support for the product. When Special Collections acquired the system, they had more staff available with responsibilities for using the system. However, due to staff attrition, remaining staff cannot devote the time required to learn and utilize the system effectively. We are open to using an alternative digital asset management system that is supported by the entire University of California system.

Unsure of what long-term costs are. Unsure of where to put the materials. Gap between best practices for digital preservation and current storage method.

Very little systematic thinking. There is no single person or unit responsible. A number of different people and/or units have been responsible for mass storage that may be utilized for long-term storage of born-digital collections. This is not a strategic priority for the institution. Mixed content. Mass storage includes important born-digital collections, surrogates of digitization projects that may or may not have long-term preservation value, and other mixed content that has not been appraised in any way. Cost carried entirely by collectors. Unlike paper storage, which is a shared library expense, digital storage expenses are allocated by the collectors. There is no current budget model that allows for the sharing of storage sufficient for born-digital collections. This is particularly a problem for special collections.

Volume of storage, we've added capacity to the system. Access to digital content is provided by DSpace. Much digital content in MASC is staff only access.

We are establishing an e-records workstation in a locked office with a secure connection to the dark archives server. Original media retained with PII will be stored in the vault used for rare books.

We benefit greatly from challenges and benefits of scale. We have local, campus-based cloud storage through centralized IT (CNS) that gives all of the benefits of cloud storage with no negatives. We are able to leverage capacity for maximized benefits.

We can't seem to get enough storage from the central IT units, and the storage we do get is doled out to us in relatively small chunks.

We have had to increase storage capabilities by working with our main IT department on a regular basis. (Particularly how our storage needs have grown substantially since first incorporating the institutional repository.)

We need to establish our preservation policy. Multiple formats and file/format stability.

18. What software/services/tools does your library currently use or plan to use for digital processing actions? Check all that apply. N=54

	Currently Use	Plan to Use	N
Open source tool (e.g., Jhove, Droid, SENF, ADAPT ACE)	31	13	44
Outsourced service (e.g., Archive-It)	12	19	31
Home-grown tool	18	11	29
Commercial tool (e.g., Aid4Mail, IdentityFinder, etc.)	21	6	27
Other software/service/tool/approach	8	5	13
Number of Responses	42	30	54

Please list the specific tool and/or briefly describe your approach (from bandaid/bootstrap approach to microservices software development) below.

Commercial tool(s) N=22

Adobe Bridge; Photoshop

Archivists Toolkit, CONTENTdm

CONTENTdm and Shared Shelf currently being used.

CONTENTdm (2 responses)

CONTENTdm for access

Currently use Adobe Pro for conversion of some documents to PDF and PDF/A, and can anticipate using other commercial products.

Forensic Tool Kit, Aid4Mail

FRED, FTK Imager

FTK; FTK Imager; ImgBurn; Aid4Mail; DVD Decrypter; Md5Checker; Catweasal ImageTool3; FC5025 Imager; ArchiveFacebook; JR Directory Printer; MediaJoin; Quick View Plus; SyncBack; Kryoflux software; PCMacLan

FTKImager (though free, proprietary), FileMerlin, Oxygen, Adobe Acrobat

Hitachi Content Platform, FAST search engine, alfresco (for our users' work environment)

Identity Finder, McAfee Anti-Virus, FTK Imager (free), EmailChemy, and QuickView Plus

IdentityFinder

Isilon enterprise storage

Mac-legacy versions of iMovie hacked into earlier versions of product (all built into the Mac OS).

OnBase by Hyland Software

Photoshop, Acrobat

Quick View Pro, FTK Imager

Symatec Backup Exec.

Use Identity Finder for PII.

We are in the very early stages of exploring the potential of SharePoint.

Open source tool(s) N=34

Archivematica (2 responses)

Archivematica (incorporates Jhove, and other open source tools)

Archivematica for preservation, ICA-AtoM for access, DSpace for access.

Archivematica, BitCurator, Hypatia, Fedora

Archivemedica: thinking about it.

Archon and Fedora

Currently, DSpace, JHOVE and GIT

Droid, Duke Data Accessioner

DROID; FITS; LOC Bagger GUI; Bagit library; Thunderbird; Handbrake; IrfanView; Shredder; WinHTTrack; YPOPs; Fiwalk; Sleuthkit; MediaInfo; Afflib; ClamAV; Fido; Archivematica; Basilisk II

DSpace currently being used; Fedora, Islandora being considered.

DSpace, ClamWinAV, JHOVE, DROID, SleuthKit

DSpace, Drupal, FEdora, Solr

DSpace, Drupal, Open Journal System

Duke Data Accessioner, Archivematica, Fedora Commons, Jhove, FITS, IRODS

Duke Data Accessioner; also looking at Archivematica.

Duraspace (Fedora Commons), ExIf tool, MediaInfo, Archivists' Toolkit, Oxygen

Evaluating Duke Data Accessioner; Archivematica; California Digital Library's Merritt; MetaArchive, etc.

Exploring archivematica or DPSP from NAA.

Fedora Commons digital repository + Hydra/Blacklight

Hydra/Fedora tools (DIL), MDID3

JHOVE, BagIT, Archivematica, AIMS, FITS, fiwalk, LOC-Bagger, Curator's Wookbench

Jhove, Droid, Archivematica, Virtualbox, HTTrack, Imgburn, CDCheck, Exiftool, + others (whatever helps/works)

Jhove, Droid, Rosetta

JHove, ImageMagick, Libraries from open source projects such as Islandora, Emory's Fedora libraries

Jhove; check sum generator; GIMP; IrfanView; Heritrix crawler; Wayback Machine web archive replay software.

Jhove; Droid

NARA File Analyzer, Duke Data Accessioner

Not yet decided

Our digital asset management system, Islandora, makes use of several open source tools. We will also be exploring how we might integrate it with Archivematica.

Sheepshaver for emulation

Starting to use Archivsts Tool kit, some use of DSspace.

ThinkUp, Yahoo2Mbox, Thunderbird, JackSummer, ADAPT ACE, aimage

Win SCP

Outsourced service N=22

Archive-It (7 responses)

California Digital Library services (Merritt repository, eScholarship, Web Archiving Service)

CDL Web Archiving Service

Considering California Digital Library Web Archiving Service for web preservation and CDL's Merritt platform.

Eventually Hathti Trust

Internet Archive.(2 responses)

Looking at Archive-It for harvesting websites.

Looking at ways to archive websites.

MetaArchive Cooperative: members, but have only used it for one collection so far and can't afford to put everything there.

Not yet decided.

Outsourced disk imaging.

Plan to contract with CDL Web Archiving Service this year.

Plan to use Archive-It's web archiving service.

Several under consideration for archiving websites.

Web Archiving Service

Home-grown tool(s) N=18

Archive-It

Bag-it; Content Transfer System (CTS); DigiBoard (nominations & permissions tool)

Check-in/ingest tool (Medical Center Archives only)

Curators' Workbench developed locally and incorporates some open source tools.

ETD Processing system, various BASH/XSLT scripts

Exploring UNC's Curator's Workbench.

Homegrown tools (more bootstrap than microservices) to interact with Fedora and use on Macs.

In the process of development.

Metadata wrapper for storage and access of digital items in Fedora.

Python-based microservices and APIs

Scripts to support accessioning and metadata extraction; Media log.

Still coming up with this maybe.

Tools for managing repository and storage network workflows.

Various Python & Perl scripts

We are customizing the open source DAMS, Islandora, to meet our requirements. See above.

We could conceivably explore home-grown tools/solutions with our university IT staff.

Workflow Management System (metadata and object handling for RUcore)

XSLT stylesheets; Schematron and RelaxNG Schemas; local scripts

Other software/service/tool/approach N=13

Archivist's Toolkit

Bagit

Considering Archivematica.

Currently exploring a variety of tools, including: checksum checkr; metadata extractor; DROID; Xena; FTK imager; Adobe Bridge.

Hand encoded MODS records

Heritrix (Web Crawling)

I do not understand the question, which indicates the problem. We work with library IT folks to whom this would mean something, hopefully.

Open source cont: DROID, Duke Data Accessioner, Apache Tika, etc.

Photoshop, Thumbs Plus, and a variety of others to carry out specific processing actions such as mass renaming; addition of caption information to each digital image lacking that information; stripping out metadata that is embedded in the header of photos and creating a text file; tools to make mass corrections of file names (for example removing all empty spaces in filenames).

SIARD

Special Collections staff personal collection of archaic software & hardware.

We acquire/develop tools as needed.

XTF, Omeka, Digital Commons, DLX, Archivists' Toolkit, Silverfast, Photoshop/CS suite, Adobe Acrobat Pro, ImageMagick, Tesseract, iMovie, Final Cut, OmniPage, ABBYY Finereader. Not sure what is being asked for this section.

ACCESS AND DISCOVERY

19. **Which of the following delivery methods does your library use to provide access to born-digital materials? Check all that apply. N=64**

For the purpose of this question, in-library access refers to a reading room or other monitored space; online access means access to materials remotely; i.e., not in a monitored space.

Online access to a digital repository system	42	66%
In-library access on dedicated computer workstation	31	48%
In-library access using portable media accessed through the users' personal computer	22	34%
Third-party access & delivery system	18	28%
Online access to a file space	15	23%
In-library access to records in an emulated environment	1	2%
Online access to records in an emulated environment	1	2%
We do not provide access at this time	13	20%
Other delivery method	10	16%

If you selected "Third-party access & delivery system" above, please specify it here. N=14

A small number of born-digital materials are included in our online CONTENTdm system, e-Archives.

Archive-It provided portal & YouSendIt

Archive-It.org, for the university web archive.

Campus-based Dropbox file sharing to send large scanned documents to distance researchers.

CONTENTdm (2 responses)

CONTENTdm for selected collections – derivatives only.

Digital repository content is syndicated to a number of online systems, including the library's VuFind catalog.

Dropbox, YouTube

LUNA Insight, CONTENTdm, ViewShare

No public interface to digital archives, so staff must provide requested digital material to researchers.

OhioLINK, but not strictly for born-digital. And once again the typical born-digital assets in OhioLINK are ETDs which are not under the purview of special collections.

Use of vendor sites for access/delivery of purchased content. Trusted partners that host parts of our digital collections.

We are in the early stages of exploring access via our Bepress/Digital Commons-based institutional repository.

If you selected "Other delivery method" above, please briefly describe it here. N=10

Ad-hoc digital libraries

Creating duplicates for patron use on storage media (CDs, DVDs).

Digital documents & images delivered to users as email attachments.

Email

Home-grown PHP app: customized file/directory browsing application

In addition to our plan to make records available online through OPA we can also deliver .zip files of assets and metadata to requesters.

We deliver all through online access whenever possible. In some cases, as with partners in different areas and countries with limited bandwidth and with materials of varying levels of extreme sensitivity, we support other modes of access as needed.

We generally do not provide access at this time, but in rare instances have provided access at a dedicated workstation in the reading room of the archives.

We pull DVD's and CD's.

We send files by the university's digital "drop box" and by email.

20. What repository system is used to manage and/or provide access to your library's born-digital materials? Check all that apply. N=63

	Manage	Provide Access	N
Open source repository software (e.g., Fedora, Archivematica, DSpace, or DAITSS)	39	33	41
None, the library uses secure file system storage	28	10	29
Commercial repository product (e.g., Rosetta)	10	12	15
Home-grown repository system	12	11	13
Other repository system	7	7	9
Number of Responses	60	53	63

If you selected "Other repository system" above, please briefly describe it here. N=14

Manage and Provide Access

CONTENTdm. Archivematica and ICA-AtoM being piloted.

Hathi Trust

Institutional records: OnBase. Personal materials: We are simply storing at the moment and not providing unmediated access due to lack of a repository for storing this material.

Shared Shelf

The original preservation copies of born-digital records are stored in a secure content management environment, the Electronic Records Archive. Those original copies are managed in archival storage and not accessed by the public. We make reference or public access copies of born-digital records and provide access to them either on hard media (for direct reference requests) or place the access versions of the files on the Online Public Access (OPA) web servers. Users can then search OPA and view and/or download the reference copies of born-digital records.

Manage

Fedora repository is under development.

Provide Access

Bepress Digital Commons

We use CONTENTdm for access. While this isn't always considered a repository system, this is the nearest fit on the survey. (We also referred to it as a repository system in question 14.)

Other Comments

CONTENTdm is used now to provide access to select born-digital materials; however, it is a short-term solution as we evaluate platforms such as Merritt that can provide both preservation and access.

Duraspace (Fedora)

Medical Center Archives does not currently have a digital repository system, but development is underway.

Open Source repository software with SobekCM

VuFind with Solr; Active Fedora stack with Blacklight, Solr

We are currently transitioning from a secure file system storage with no access to a Fedora-based repository system.

21. Are different types of repositories used for different types of born-digital materials? N=60

Yes	38	63%
No	22	37%

If yes, please briefly describe which type of repository is used for which type of material. N=36

A locally created web-based access system is used for the University Curriculum Archive, which is a mix of digitized and born-digital content.

Archival electronic records both via file system server and DSpace.

Archive-It serves as a commercial repository product for web-archived material. DSpace, and open-source repository software, is used to provide access to some open materials that can be described at the item level. The rest is managed via file storage.

Bepress (commercial) used for institutional repository; open source plans for Special Collections.

CONTENTdm is used for searching and access. DSpace is used for dark archives (the Institutional Repository).

Currently, two instances of DSpace are used to deliver some born-digital content.

DSpace for thesis and dissertations and some university electronic content; a secure limited access sever space for digital content, such as mpeg movie files, created in MASC digitization projects.

Described above: Archive-It for web archive; DSpace for ETDs; file system storage for other born-digital special collections materials.

DSpace for GIS data; CONTENTdm for documents, audio, visual materials.

DSpace for ETDs. Shared Shelf for photographs and artworks.

DSpace handles our institutional and subject repositories and is primarily a text and data focused site. UMedia Archive (Drupal, Fedora) is used to manage and present our rich media and image files.

DSpace is currently used for the output of the university's research community, e.g., theses and dissertations, datasets. Islandora, our digital asset management system, is used for all other forms of digital content and will be utilized for born-digital records too. Archivematica will also be investigated with regards to processing and managing born-digital content with ICA-AtoM providing access.

DSpace is used as the platform for our institutional repository; we will be using a Fedora-based system for our long-term digital preservation repository.

DSpace is used for our institutional repository; CONTENTdm is used for material digitized in the library; ICA-AtoM is used for collected born-digital material.

DSpace is used for traditional digital objects that DSpace usually manages. Everything else is not in DSpace.

DSpace: theses, DTDs. Homegrown: digital photographs, film, etc.

Fedora is used as basis for dark archive for all materials. DSpace is used as repository and for access to mostly textual materials. Other systems are used for access to images, video, etc. Materials will be stored in Fedora-based repository.

Fedora system used for digital collections and images; VuFind - selective content including some e-text;

For institutional records we are using OnBase an ECM system. We are still figuring out how to handle personal materials. OnBase may be our solution, though likely it will not be.

Images in LUNA Insight, documents in DSpace.

Institutional repository.

Manuscript vs. University Records.

Most files are kept on disk space managed by the Carolina Digital Repository, but extremely large or numerous files are kept on a tape-based storage system.

Not within Special Collections, but other units in the library are using other systems (Bepress, Luna).

Secure file system storage and Fedora are for dark archive material and deep storage. Fedora use is still in test stages, so it may also be used for access copies of digital content at a future time.

The institutional repository (DSpace) manages simple files. Secure file systems storage is used for complex datasets with access through DSpace. CONTENTdm manages curated special collections.

There are three repositories currently in use, although none of them are recommended for preservation, only access. The Libraries uses CONTENTdm for access to born-digital archives and special collections (e-Archives), the NanoHub for access to born-digital faculty research data sets (PURR-Purdue University Research Repository), and Digital Commons from Bepress (e-Pubs) as an institutional repository for access to faculty research articles, pre-prints, electronic theses and dissertations, etc.

Theses and dissertations repository provided by library consortia uses DSpace. Everything else managed on original media and/or file system storage.

We can't put everything in our Access digital repository. Collections such as copyright protected sound recordings, audiovisual material, sound files are only available on a case-by-case basis in-house or through limited time hosting platform (Omeka exhibit).

We have Scholar Commons for access to faculty documents that are born-digital and we have CONTENTdm that might be used for born-digital library collections, but has not really yet. There are a few films and oral histories in CONTENTdm, but that database is not for preservation, just access.

We manage preservation and access of books digitized by Google and Microsoft in Hathi Trust.

We use a Digital Asset Management system to catalog and manage multi-media material (mostly photographs and some audio and video). This system is for back-end use only. We export from it to other delivery systems as appropriate. We use a DSpace repository for our text-based, born-digital archival materials as well as for some content exported from our DAMS. The California Digital Library's Web Archiving Service is used for managing web-based content.

We use an institutional repository to manage scholarly content, CONTENTdm for managing our digital collections and OJS for managing journal content.

We're moving from scattered RAIDs, servers, etc. to the Isilon.

While we don't currently use different repository systems, Special Collections/University Archives plans to purchase an electronic records management system in the near future, which will probably be a commercial system independent of the library's Fedora repository. However, records of scholarly value that can be made openly available will be shared with RUcore.

22. Please briefly describe up to three challenges your library has faced in providing access to born-digital materials (e.g., arrangement and description, copyright, confidential content, etc.) and how the library has addressed that challenge. N=53

Access and Discovery Challenges Word Cloud

Ability to manage access based on a wide and changing variety of licensing and access restrictions. Technical infrastructure to manage access to restricted content beyond our IP range has not yet been developed. The policies and tools for authenticating off-site users have not been developed.

Adopting/developing descriptive standards and standard workflows for describing born-digital materials. Integrating descriptions of born-digital materials with analog materials. Handling confidential materials with appropriate access controls.

All manual process. We do not have a digital repository system that enables us to provide access to born-digital collections over the Internet. Most access must be provided on-site on non-networked computers. This is an inefficient, cumbersome, and slow process. Skilled staff are responsible for setting up computers upon patron request. Limited description. At this point, only some staff are comfortable describing born-digital collections. This leads to limited description of those collections that may be limiting use. Also, lack of appropriate tools to undertake description, particularly in the past. There is no infrastructure to manage user permissions (if there were an online access system).

Appropriate platforms to manage and deliver content (work in progress).

Arrangement and description of born-digital materials is an ongoing challenge, since current practices were developed primarily to deal with non-digital materials. Our new Digital Special Collections Librarian will be tasked with developing best practices for arrangement and amending current description practices to suit born-digital materials. Provincial privacy legislation creates challenges in providing access to born-digital university archives. This challenge may be addressed over time through implementation of a university recordkeeping metadata standard, which will facilitate management of university archives according to the security classification of these records. The previously described issue of using multiple systems to manage and provide access to born-digital materials is another challenge, which will be addressed through future development of a library digital repository to rationalize storage and access, and also federated search tools to facilitate searching across multiple systems, when necessary.

Arrangement and description, processing.

Arrangement and description are the primary challenges to access and discovery. Born-digital materials arrive on legacy media with scant metadata to inform development of effective finding aids.

Arrangement and description of legacy material is a challenge because the media was managed as a physical item and arranged into one series, when the content may intellectually belong to a number of different series. We need to modify our gift agreement to clarify what kind of online access we can provide to born-digital material acquired from external parties (web access, library-only access, etc.) and also address the technological challenge of restricting access.

Arrangement and description; technical skills commitment from institution. Copyright and privacy; lack of policies and procedures. No good sustainable delivery mechanism.

Arrangement and description: collecting particular metadata up front; knowing what to collect (what subject experts or users might want plus what programmers will need—and how to crosswalk those elements); much manipulation of web display elements. File management-naming standards, organization, quality control, migrating files from DLI to Tech Services to Systems Programmers to Archive. Discovery and searchability of our digital collections, including Trace repository—OAI, OCR, finding aids, etc., as well as copyright issues.

Arrangement and description. The library provides simple searchable metadata records through the institutional repository. However, not all metadata is represented in these records.

Confidential content. We have records that are restricted for up to 10 years by the donor and have closed the entire collection until we are able to provide access only to the open content in a manner in which it cannot be altered by users. Copyright. We may not wish to make the full copy of an item available, or to make it available at a useable resolution. Remote access to large files. We've used Dropbox in some instances.

Copyright. Arrangement and description—currently focused on developing program.

Copyright: collection donor does not have copyright over content. Arrangement and description is not in line with the analog part of the collection, it is done separately and sometimes well after we have provided access to paper based materials. Time: we often focus on digitizing collections and providing access to those before we can work with the born-digital content.

Copyright: attempt to reach agreements with providers/publishers. Creating relevant descriptive metadata: metadata librarian supervises student workers. Development of access interface: Libraries are piloting Islandora, Archives are in the process of developing access interface.

Copyright and confidential content. We are investigating the applicability of the "one item one user" model that would limit access to copyrighted material to one authenticated user at a time. Similar to checking out a book or document in the reading room. Levels of granularity. Users expect item level access (or beyond) how do we describe this content in a meaningful way? We are exploring automated metadata creation tools such as document analysis.

Copyright and licensing. Consistency in user entered metadata.

Copyright: we use systems that allow very granular control of permissions and access. Privacy: we have policies governing access to confidential records, but procedures specific to born-digital materials are still being developed. We hope to use systems that allow very granular control of permissions and access.

Copyright: copyright statement in tagged metadata. Software upgrade/migration: purchasing new software and hardware. Limiting access to private collections: through software, some collections are only accessible in-house or through restricted IP.

Copyright: might actually be less of an issue than with some of our legacy analog collections, but people send digital content without deeds of gift just as they do analog collections. We've had some success with getting people to agree to CC licenses. Limited resources for development and support of repository, digital collection management system, etc.: we do not have as much programming support as we would like, for example. We do the best we can with what we have, maintaining a commitment to standards and trying to preserve what is essential about both context and content. Arrangement and description: image filenames assigned by creators (or their cameras) can be meaningless and/or misleading, particularly when they are presented to the public as the identifier for ordering a copy of the image. In cases like this, where the original filenames were not essential or meaningful, we have renamed files. We have not yet received a collection that contains a significant amount of textual digital content; we anticipate different but substantial issues when we get to that frontier.

Copyright: we have required users to log in in order to access materials subject to copyright protection. User experience: presently, there are a number of access methods and systems in place that are not integrated. Users need to move between the disparate systems and understand how to use each system in order to encounter different parts of a single collection. We seek a solution that will be an easier way to integrate the experience into one interface. Managing access levels: we would like more access control granularity than we presently have. Rather than having collections accessible to all of the world, or all of those on the campus network or with a login. We have not yet begun discussions about how to address this issue.

Copyright. Workflow, including arrangement and description. Preservation.

Currently, materials are not in an organized database that is accessible online or easy for users to access while at the library, so basically materials that are born-digital are not really accessible at all.

Describing the large volume of born-digital materials in a scalable and practical way. To address this challenge, we are exploring the possibility of adding high level or accession level "preliminary descriptions" to the online catalog, before the records have been processed by archival staff. This applies to both born-digital records as well as traditional records. We need a better understanding of how to effectively index, search, and render results for the large volume (petabytes) of born-digital and digitized records, for a large variety of file formats. We are aiming to address this challenge by seeking assistance from a search expert to help us optimize search and display of electronic records in our online catalog. Reviewing the large volume of born-digital materials for access or use restrictions prior to making them available. The current review model and workflow is not scalable or sustainable. This challenge has not yet been addressed.

Determining how to collection and to manage born-digital materials. Determining staff resources for management of born-digital materials. Determining funding needs and resources for management of born-digital materials.

Development of an interface for patron access. Copyright. Confidential/restricted content.

Donor restrictions requiring in-house use only: in-house provision, despite user unhappiness. Copyright: take down notices, disclaimers, risk assessment.

For personal materials, the lack of a repository. We have not adequately addressed this issue.

How to deal with materials that are under copyright or otherwise of a more restricted nature. Our current systems are intended to support an open model of preservation to access. We are beginning to address the divergent needs for archive space with limited or no access and how best to manage it. We are also evaluating our collecting policies to ensure they align with our digital acquisitions. How do we balance the need to support access to our collections with the restrictive mandates that might be required under copyright or donor agreements?

How to present digital objects in a standardized fashion or to be able to save/render legacy and/or complex formats. We have only just begun to address these challenges on a piecemeal and ad hoc basis.

Lack of a repository suited for easy upload/ingest of born-digital materials with additional tools available for supporting preservation metadata. Staff resources/time to describe born-digital materials, prepare them for uploading into an access system, particularly regarding creation of preservation metadata and other descriptive metadata. Restrictions placed by donors or by law on access to some born-digital archives and special collections, which need to be maintained in a repository but without access for a period of time.

Limited staff.

Managing permissions for various types of users (distance researchers, classes of students, faculty, TAs, etc.), which can change, are time sensitive, need to be secure. Large files can crash our server or significantly slow down the system. Structure and display of files.

Metadata: we lack full-featured metadata creation and management systems for descriptive, rights, administrative, and structural metadata. Poor solutions in the past. We are currently in the process of adapting the new Hypatia libraries on our Fedora platform. Copyright, permissions, privacy: we are working through these issues as they arise. Scaling up our operation to accommodate born-digital archival collections and other born-digital special collections may be slowed down by the need to investigate rights status, clear rights, and do risk analyses. Software development: working in the open source Fedora environment has many advantages but does require significant local investment in software development. When possible we are leveraging others' work with Fedora, Hypatia, and Blacklight and contributing code to those projects.

One of the top challenges right now for providing access to born-digital material is the inadequacy of our current descriptive tools (EAD and MARC) and their discovery and display interfaces to deal with the nature of born-digital content. The scale of the born-digital content easily overwhelms the traditional library catalog-style digital library interface (1 record per item) and the EAD record is not created or managed in a way that can take advantage of the born-digital components either (too many items to list or link them all; the text and technical metadata for objects doesn't have a container in EAD). The Hypatia project, as part of the AIMS grant, worked on ways to build interaction between these systems so that the individual digital objects can be managed in an appropriate repository environment, but discovery of them can be integrated with description of non-digital components in a finding aid. We are still working on developing this kind of system locally. A major issue related to born-digital material is restrictions on access both due to sensitive or private information and intellectual property rights. They are related, but slightly different issues. Sensitive and private information is restricted from all view unless permission is granted. In order to provide this information then we would need to grant access to some users but not to others. In some cases this would be access granted to a class of user (university affiliates), but in other cases it would be on a case-by-case basis. Issues then would be being able to identify and remove, redact, or restrict the appropriate content (not always easy to do) and to grant access to appropriate individuals. Eventually, we would like for all content to be managed through a digital repository, so that will mean that we will need some sophisticated authentication controls. Issues related to intellectual property arise due to the fact that we do not own copyright to the majority of the material we collect. When we just provided access to paper copies that were difficult to reproduce in the reading room to a single user at a time, this access was considered well within fair use. If we were to simply make access available to born-digital content online to anyone we would have dramatically changed the situation: now copying is easy and multiple people can see the content. This would increase our risk of overreaching fair use. As a way to avoid this, we will make some digital materials available only in our reading room on a dedicated computer used only for viewing content, not copying or taking notes. A third challenge is related again to the software formats of much of the born-digital content. We suspect that most users will want to use a modern file format, especially for materials that we can make widely available on the web. In addition, we will not be able to find and support every software needed to view every file type in our own reading room for those materials only available there. For some formats, we know we can migrate to an acceptable access format (modern PDFs can be derived from early Microsoft Word formats), but for others there is no clear migration path. In addition, there will be some number of researchers who will want access to the original formats. This would mean that we would need to be able to get reasonably quick access to both a normalized access format as well as the original.

One significant challenge continues to be donor restrictions and copyright issues. For now, we are only providing access to the material within the reading room. We also would like to add a more advanced set of tools for researchers to use while interacting with the born-digital collections. Our current approach is to solicit feedback from researchers and develop plans for future tool development.

Organizing and describing research data was a significant challenge, but we believe we have developed a methodology that uses events to describe research context and RDF relationships to link resources within a research project together. We have also developed a research data application profile that enables us to provide core descriptions of research data to enable interdisciplinary reuse of data. We are working to resolve the challenge of collection level description, using EAD, within the RUcore repository. We are developing a context object methodology that uses relationship metadata to link resources and that creates generic "core" metadata at the object level, so that individual objects do not need to be described individually. We do not currently have a methodology for describing and managing websites, but are hoping that the EAD methodology, which supports hierarchical relationships, can be used to manage the more matrix-like site maps of websites.

Our ingest and storage system is brand new and partially still in the planning stage; discovery and access tools are still in development. The library is presently building a Hydra/Fedora institutional repository structure and access to born-digital records in a primary use case.

Overall processing workflows and workloads: this is related to the earlier challenge of insufficient staffing. In the short-term, we are incorporating these responsibilities along with the other primary responsibilities of existing staff. Arrangement and description: this is related to the earlier challenge of insufficient staffing. In the short-term, we are incorporating these responsibilities along with the other primary responsibilities of existing staff. Access for reference service: this is related to the earlier challenge of insufficient staffing. In the short-term, we are incorporating these responsibilities along with the other primary responsibilities of existing staff.

Processing efficiently. For physical materials, we are adopting efficient processing procedures where we organize, appraise, describe, and house materials in less and less granular ways. However, for the first few born-digital collections we processed, we found that we had to work at the item or file level. This may be because the files were from floppy disks with no discernible original order or series. An archivist had to open up, evaluate, and provide a descriptive title for every file/item. She also reviewed the material for confidentiality issues. This level of processing is not sustainable, and we are actively looking for other methods to automate this work. Many of our born-digital collections are faculty papers and contain the same sorts of files that physical faculty papers contain: collected articles authored by other individuals, letters of recommendation for colleagues, drafts of unpublished books, etc. If we provided access to these freely on the web, we might be in violation of copyright, or we might violate individuals' reasonable expectation for privacy, or we might hamper the family's ability to publish works posthumously. We developed the concept of a Virtual Reading Room so that we could provide remote access to this content online in the same way as we do to physical items in our physical reading room. While the metadata for the material is exposed publicly, you have to enter the Virtual Reading Room in order to view the content of the files. The full-text is not indexed in Google either, thus protecting the individuals about whom correspondence is written. To enter, we require that researchers complete the same application we would have them complete if they came into our physical reading room. They sign off on a copyright statement as a condition of using the material. The Virtual Reading Room is providing a layer of risk mitigation by doing three things: 1) It shows that our intent is to provide access for educational, personal, or research purposes only, just like we have always done for similar, analog materials in our reading room. 2) It makes use of the material conditional upon users agreeing to only use the material for educational, personal, or research purposes. 3) It shifts some of the accountability for violating fair use to the user.

Providing interfaces to allow users to set access controls, and managing access to non-public items in various systems. The variety of formats and complex objects that require special user interface programming. Displaying complex objects in search results.

Restrictions: our digital asset management system is designed to be used by all units on campus, not just Libraries/ Archives. Restrictions will have to be able to be applied at unit, user, item, and collection levels. Libraries IT staff is currently working on enabling this function of the system. Archival context: while our digital content resides in our digital asset management system, archival descriptions are located in ICA-AtoM. Libraries is planning on linking the two systems together to demonstrate the provenancial and archival context of the digital items. Metadata creation: all metadata linked to digital content is created by contract digitization technicians. While the Libraries has been successful in acquiring funding for this very important task, there is no baseline funding in the Libraries budget for this type of metadata creation.

Sensitive data: we have yet to work out issues surrounding born-digital institutional records with restricted access, e.g., promotion & tenure files, president's office files, etc. Graduate school policy resists open access to electronic theses and dissertations in the institutional repository.

The basic issue of how to provide access, particularly for things that are copied to our server since that is not publicly accessible. Address is by providing access on CD or flash drive, but that requires much advance work before the patron comes. For the few collections we have that have digital content, determining and then conveying to patrons now through description what we have in analog format vs. digital format, or in both analog and digital. In practice, we provide varying levels of description about the digital content and do not always go to the extent to determine what we have in digital form vs. analog. Easily generating file lists: WordPerfect used to do this easily, Word does not.

There are concerns about our ability to provide copies of our digital content without violating copyright. We are currently reviewing existing donor agreements to evaluate what rights we have. Discovery of our digital materials is poor. EAD does not lend itself well to describing the digital materials and we do not have a metadata browse/search/discovery tool that permits a combination of item-level and aggregate description. There are concerns regarding our ability to provide original files v. derivative versions (due to redaction and/or migration) and informing potential users about both/either of the options.

Theses and dissertations: copyright issues. This is partly addressed by providing embargo options for our theses and dissertations.

Training for staff on how to arrange and describe born-digital materials. We are working to bring appropriate training to the library and to our region. Managing collections with personal identifiable information. We are trying to determine what the best strategy is for providing access to these materials and don't have a good answer. Managing user rights for restricted collections. We are investigating this as part of our Rosetta pilot project.

Unclear copyright status; verifying copyright status!!! Metadata arrangements need more standardization. How to effectively integrate into basic discovery systems.

We continue to look at methods of display for special materials (such as newer file formats, book reader (page turner) and also incorporating other metadata to support these materials (TEI, MODS). Copyright: certain materials in the institutional repository are only available with university credentials due to copyright issues.

We face the challenge of separating out confidential material. Digital access is not currently provided to collections containing this content.

We have no policies or mechanisms for delivering born-digital content at this time.

Without a Digital Asset Management System (DAMS) in place we have not been able to provide access/discovery. A current system-wide initiative is working on a solution to this. Rights management issues and a clear understanding of what materials can be made available have hindered access. System-wide initiative is currently working on a solution.

Working out issues relating to security/privacy (as mentioned above).

USE POLICY

23. Are the born-digital materials your library offers or plans to offer available to all library users or is their use restricted to certain categories of users? N=63

Some born-digital materials are available to all users; other materials are restricted	52	83%
All born-digital materials are available to all users	8	13%
Use is restricted to certain categories of users	3	5%

Please briefly describe any restrictions on the use of born-digital materials (e.g., user category, institutional affiliation, internal policy such as restriction on personnel, student-related records, etc.) N=52

Some born-digital materials are available to all users; other materials are restricted

Access restrictions may be stipulated in donor agreements, for special collections materials. Provincial privacy legislation restricts access to university archives containing personal information. The university's IP policy allows broader use and reproduction of some copyrighted materials by the university community than by external users.

As mentioned previously, our system will enable born-digital materials to be restricted by unit, user, collection, and item.

As per our normal practices, restrictions may apply if required by the donor and/or privacy laws.

At the moment, largely donor-imposed.

Based on already existing policies for restrictions regarding institutional and organization records.

Certain records are restricted per university records access policy, regardless of format.

Confidentiality.

Deed of gift restricts some materials.

Depends on the content. Items can be restricted to individuals or to specific IP ranges.

Digital materials may be subject to the same sorts of restrictions as analog materials: law (FERPA, etc.), university records policies, and donor-imposed restrictions. There are no restrictions unique to digital materials.

FERPA or other privacy laws, copyright, IPR, internal hierarchical operations, donor restrictions.

FERPA-based as well as institutional policy.

Institution affiliation for electronic theses and dissertations.

Just like any other collection that might have restrictions.

Licenses or agreement restrictions.

Like any material in our collection, some will have restrictions on access, determined by the deed of gift. Otherwise, all content will be available to anyone, although material for which we do not own copyright will most likely only be available by physically visiting the reading room.

Materials may be restricted based on donor agreements, state records laws, privacy considerations, and university policies and regulations.

Materials where we hold copyright and not subject to restrictions (primarily university records content previously released to the public & web-content) are available online. Other materials, where there is uncertainty regarding copyright, are accessible locally. Still other materials are restricted as per donor agreements or to protect SEI.

Materials that we own the copyright to we distribute freely. Other items might be made available to researchers for purposes of private research and personal use after signing a researcher agreement with the university.

Only user restrictions would be copyright and need to clear use with owner of images, as well as any security classified (these are both access and use restricted) restrictions that may pertain to certain images in an accession.

Restrictions are based on user category. Some restricted institutional materials may only be open to certain categories of users from the university.

Restrictions based on federal law, donor requests, type of record.

Restrictions based on information content, just like all other archives.

Restrictions can be for reasons of copyright, contract law, or privacy. Different collections or material types raise different issues. Our informal categories of access are: world-readable, on-campus access, on-site access, access by permission for research, and access only by content owners or curatorial staff.

Restrictions might include issues related to access or copyright. Personal data would be further restricted as would any donor-level agreements.

Restrictions on personnel and student records.

Restrictions on some born-digital materials include: lack of copyright to make the content available freely online; donor restriction for a period of time due to sensitivity of information in the materials; legal restrictions to content, such as documents containing personally identifiable information relating to medical treatment, etc.

Restrictions on student-related information protected by FERPA. Restrictions on embargoed material.

Some faculty data sets deposited to the digital repository have restrictions.

Some items restricted to on campus only.

Some materials are restricted to university-only access because they are student-related records, have copyright restrictions, etc. Some records held by the Medical Center Archives contain PHI and are protected under the HIPAA Privacy Rule and the HIPAA Security Rule.

Some materials may be restricted as a result of policies and/or regulations, or donor agreements.

Some materials *may* be restricted to non-community users, perhaps. As of now, everything is open to everyone and we will try to keep that status as long as we can.

Some material may be restricted to on-campus use only (i.e., in library or reading room) or to members of the campus community (i.e., faculty, staff, students).

The dark archive is accessible to library staff only. Born-digital materials have the same access restrictions as their analog predecessors. Graduate school policy resists open access to ETDs. Researchers deny open access to data collections.

The format of the records has not changed who we make records available to. Our standard user categories (i.e., university staff, researchers, etc.) still apply.

The restrictions would be the same as we have for paper records—restrict personnel or student-related data, donor restrictions.

The same restrictions that apply to paper documents will apply to born-digital materials. We have a five-page access policy governing these issues that I cannot restate here.

There are internal policies relating to personnel, such as university personnel records containing personal information.

University records are restricted for a set time period and then open to the public. However, the creating office has access to the records during the restriction period. The restrictions vary depending on the nature of the creating office. We also have some collections that are restricted based on donor request.

University records are restricted to certain staff. Some manuscript collections carry restrictions to certain categories of users. However, most collections are open to all users.

User category.

User category and institutional affiliation.

Varying restriction periods on certain types of records (institutional records, personnel, student) and potential other restrictions per individual gift agreements.

We embargo some resources, such as ETDs and research data, at the request of the student or faculty member. These embargoes generally represent a desire to finish a research project, publish a book or article on the findings, etc. We will also restrict parts of a research project indefinitely if the data has privacy issues.

All born-digital materials are available to all users

All content is available to all users; however, not all content is available on the web.

As a public institution, institutional records are available for public scrutiny within certain exceptions outlined in law. Any other restrictions would be dictated by donor agreements. There are no uniform restrictions, and we have such a minimal amount of born-digital materials right now there are not any identifiable categories.

Copyright and university policy are the main restrictions for the content we have collected to date.

Use is restricted to certain categories of users

For current processed content, only MARBL users who have registered with MARBL and have access to the researcher workstation in the reading room can use born-digital materials.

Restrictions based on internal policy.

Some of our born-digital collections are available only in a Virtual Reading Room. To gain access to our Virtual Reading Room, all researchers must submit an application to use a collection and agree to follow our rules of use. So long as researchers do this, they may use the materials.

24. **Does your library require users to complete any registration process before using born-digital materials? N=60**

Yes	25	42%
No	35	58%

If registration is required, please briefly describe the process. N=34

Answered Yes

All on-site users register at first visit, regardless of what materials they are using.

All researchers who use MARBL content must first register. Researchers fill out a questionnaire, show identification, and have a brief orientation/interview with Research Services staff.

All special collections users complete the same registration process (using Aeon system). No additional registration, unless required for a particular collection.

All users who visit our reading room are required to register by showing a valid form of ID and filling out a registration form (users who are affiliated with the university are pre-registered through our university's authentication system). Since many materials will be available only in the reading room, users will need to register before use. We are exploring the idea of making other materials available freely to university users from any location through a login, or making material available through campus networks, but those uses have not been fully worked out and may not be viable or needed.

Currently, it still is a paper process. We are developing a "click through" approach in the new repository environment.

Currently, we use the same registration process required for physical manuscript collections. The user fills out the appropriate paperwork and then has an interview with one of our curators. This has been fairly easy to enforce because the born-digital materials currently held in special collections are used in our reading room. There is no equivalent registration process for the born-digital materials in our digital collections, institutional repository, or open journal system. We have other born-digital materials that may not be accessed without the permission of the principal investigator of the research project that the materials pertain to.

Fill out contract outlining what you want access to. Researcher assumes liability should they republish or distribute the material. Once signed form is returned or payment received (cost of digitizing an analog recording, photograph, etc.) we provide the copies or access.

If born-digital materials contain sensitive data, researchers may be required to apply to the Institutional Review Board to gain access.

In the Rare Book and Manuscript Library, registration is done through standard Rare Book registration procedure. Elsewhere within the library system it is via informal request to curatorial staff or administrators. This will continue to vary depending on the type of material or collection, its nature, and its custodial location.

Materials available online via DSpace or Archive-It do not require user registration. All other materials require a user to register on-site as per our default researcher policy.

Normal archives patron registration process.

Normal registration process.

Patron registration form.

Reader registration and being on-site at the library is required to access all restricted collections.

Registration through paper form is required of all users. Special Collections and Archives staff enter the information into a restricted database and shred the paper forms.

Required to fill out online registration form and note which collection they are accessing.

Same as for all SC/A materials.

Same as for on-site use of any special collections.

Since all access is on-site (except for some oral histories), they would undergo the same reader registration process required for users of paper collections. Processed oral histories that were originally recorded digitally (not digitized from analog tape) are available without registration in the Louisiana Digital Library, a CONTENTdm site.

The same as we would for paper materials.

They complete the standard Patron Use form that all users complete.

Users fill out a form. After completing it, staff review it and allow researchers to create an account in our DSpace system to access the material. The registration applies only to born-digital materials that we put into our Virtual Reading Room, due to copyright or confidentiality issues. Some of our born-digital material is open to all users online.

We are rarely able to make born-digital materials accessible, but when we do, patrons must complete the same registration process as patrons using papers in our reading room.

While we cannot provide access at this time, access to born-digital records for onsite users will require registration.

Yes, the same as any other user.

Answered No

Haven't thought about that.

However, on-site researchers have to register into the research rooms and on-site researchers using a library-provided computer have to register use of that computer, but not to access born-digital materials per se.

Not for materials in the IR or on the open web, but if made available only within special collections, the same registration process that applies to all users would be used. A paper form is filled out, and the researcher must provide photo ID.

Traditional methods of registration include library accounts and registration upon entering the archives. Online methods include IP range restriction, Shibboleth authentication, and tracking from web analytics such as Google Analytics.

We don't, but this is an interesting thought, and we may.

Will depend on the materials.

With online access no, but if one is using the object in the reading room, there is a registration process.

Other Comments

It would depend. Not for our LUNA collections, but if we allowed in-reading room use, yes.

We will be exploring this issue at a later time and cannot provide a response until our exploration of this topic concludes.

ADDITIONAL COMMENTS

25. Please submit any additional information about processing and managing born-digital materials at your institution that may assist the authors in accurately analyzing the results of this survey. N=20

As much as possible we treat all archival content the same way in terms of policies and procedures. For born-digital the main differences are technological issues that are mainly internal and do not affect patron policies.

For university institutional records, the Records Manager will be heavily influential in acquiring born-digital materials that are authentic and reliable by working with creators before records are created and will have to work closely with Archives staff in ensuring their authenticity and reliability are preserved during their transfer to archival custody.

In early stages of managing born-digital materials beyond basic content such as e-dissertations and theses. Currently assessing future directions for growing born-digital collections, including many of the questions raised in this survey.

Libraries and Archives both report to CIO. Digital curation approached differently due to different missions, but Libraries and Archives collaborate where we can.

Other than ingest, access, and preservation issues, we don't treat born-digital materials any differently than we do paper materials. We intend to apply the same policies and procedures to born-digital materials wherever possible.

Policies and practices differ across special collections units within the library, although our collaboration is increasing as we seek to find shared solutions. Variances in practice are clarified in comments throughout the survey.

Processing and management of born-digital materials in the library and across the university has been somewhat fragmented, developing within functional "silos" over time. Current campus-wide information systems planning initiatives and also strategic planning within the library will reduce this fragmentation of effort and facilitate future management and larger-scale ingest of born-digital special collections and university archives materials. One important aspect of these initiatives will probably be the development of digital repositories that can be used by different groups within the university with similar storage and access needs.

Separate from Special Collections, the institutional repository ingests research data, non-commercial e-only publications, and electronic theses and dissertations.

The processing and management of born-digital materials is currently done on an ad hoc basis. We are working to create procedures and policies to institutionalize our practice but there is little literature to use as a basis for this.

This survey is very timely as we have had two recent potential donors want to give born-digital material to the South Carolina Political Collections (SCPC) archive and the special collections librarians have begun talking about these very issues. We are in the early stages of creating policies and strategies for preservation and access, but we know we need to. SCPC has already acquired a fair amount of legacy media and electronic files, but the South Caroliniana Library and Rare Books are not far behind in collecting born-digital materials as well.

We are acquiring digital content, but not in great volumes: a few primarily analog collections have come in with floppy disks, CDs, etc., we have received a few born-digital photograph collections, we preserve some born-digital university records (including photographs) and community publications, we work with ETDs, and we have preserved some community-related web content via Archive-It.

We are at the early stage of development in terms of process flow and content management. Very little has been operationalized. Different types of born-digital material (e.g., e-archives, web archives, research data, audio and video oral histories) have different requirements, staffing needs, timetables, etc., and will necessarily have different workflows and ingest routes.

We are currently building the IT staff capacity to help support the digital library/archives initiatives.

We are currently in a transition phase. We have newly created positions and new hires (e.g., Digital Archivist) brought in to more pointedly better address issues/challenges of collecting, managing, preserving, and delivering born-digital and digitized content.

We are farther ahead working with materials in the digital repository than working with archives and special collections. Archives and Special Collections was not part of the digital repository development or the selection of materials to place there until very recently.

We are in the process of moving management of our digital collections as a series of separate projects to a program-based coordinated approach across the institution. Institutional archives are collected and managed through the Office of the Librarian.

We are still in the very early stages of determining how to manage born-digital materials. This survey has provided much food for thought.

We have begun planning for everything mentioned in this survey, but have really only begun implementation. I've answered the questions based on what our plans are, but in many cases we have not actually completed implementing these plans.

RESPONDING INSTITUTIONS

University of Arizona
Arizona State University
Brigham Young University
University of British Columbia
Brown University
University of Calgary
University of California, Irvine
University of California, Riverside
University of California, San Diego
Case Western Reserve University
University of Chicago
University of Colorado at Boulder
Columbia University
University of Connecticut
Cornell University
Dartmouth College
Duke University
Emory University
University of Florida
George Washington University
Georgia Institute of Technology
University of Illinois at Urbana-Champaign
Iowa State University
Johns Hopkins University
University of Kansas
Kent State University
University of Kentucky
Library of Congress
Louisiana State University
University of Louisville
University of Manitoba
University of Massachusetts, Amherst

Massachusetts Institute of Technology
Michigan State University
University of Minnesota
University of Missouri
Université de Montréal
National Archives and Records Administration
University of Nebraska–Lincoln
University of New Mexico
University of North Carolina at Chapel Hill
North Carolina State University
Northwestern University
University of Notre Dame
Ohio University
Ohio State University
Oklahoma State University
Pennsylvania State University
Purdue University
Rutgers University
University of South Carolina
Southern Illinois University Carbondale
University at Buffalo, SUNY
Syracuse University
Temple University
University of Tennessee
Texas Tech University
University of Virginia
Washington State University
Washington University in St. Louis
University of Waterloo
University of Western Ontario
Yale University
York University

REPRESENTATIVE DOCUMENTS

Job Descriptions

DIGITAL ARCHIVIST
RARE BOOK & MANUSCRIPT LIBRARY, COLUMBIA UNIVERSITY

The Columbia University Rare Book & Manuscript Library (RBML) seeks a skilled and accomplished electronic records archivist to help design and implement a curatorial and archival program for born-digital materials. While this position is in the RBML, it will work with all of Columbia's special collections units in developing and coordinating a robust and consistent archival program for born digital materials.

Reporting to the Curator of Manuscripts and University Archivist, the Digital Archivist is responsible for identifying and managing born digital content in RBML collections.

Characteristic duties and responsibilities include:

- Develops and maintains file plans, retention schedules, procedure manuals and guides to support the effective collection and management of born digital content;

- Takes the lead in helping develop policies and technical standards for digital content creators, both within Columbia and within the professional archival community;

- Works with the University Archivist to survey campus departments, offices, and website for University digital assets of enduring legal, administrative, and historical value;

- Collaborates with the staff of the Libraries Digital Programs Division on the design and functional requirements for an electronic archives management and preservation system;

- Serves as the resource person for Columbia's special collections on evolving standards and best practices for born digital content management and administration;

- Keeps statistics and prepares regular reports on manuscript and archival processing; supports and participates in RBML reference and public service. Participates in unit-wide planning and committee activities;

Requirements
- MLS from ALA-accredited library school or the equivalent in theory and practice. Graduate work in the humanities or social sciences;

- Demonstrated knowledge of digital archival and record management theory and practice. Minimum 2 years experience in the acquisition, management, and curation of born digital assets (or equivalent combination of education and experience);

- Demonstrated familiarity with data structure standards relevant to the archival control of digital collection materials (EAD, Dublin Core, MODS);

- Working knowledge of XML and digital content creation/transformation tools;

- Knowledge of DACS archival descriptive standard;

- Basic familiarity with automated library information management systems, such as Voyager, and other online union catalogs such as WorldCat;

- Demonstrated ability to communicate effectively, both orally and in writing;

- Demonstrated ability to work independently as well as collaboratively in a production-oriented, rapidly changing environment; and ability to meet project goals and deadlines.

****

Archivist I
Electronic Records Archivist

Responsibilities: The Electronic Records Archivist I is responsible for developing and implementing workflows and processes enabling the effective acquisition, description, access, management and preservation of a broad range of digital content, including university records, websites, email, and personal digital archives. Reporting to the Director of the University Archives & Historical Collections, this position works closely with other archivists, librarians, information technologists and records creators throughout the university.

The Electronic Records Archivist I will manage day-to-day activities in conjunction with the development and management of repository services, the web archiving program, and a wide variety of born-digital records ingest and access initiatives. The archivist will take the lead in identifying digital records of continuing institutional value and in developing strategies for long-term preservation and access. The archivist will be expected to remain current with emerging standards and professional best practices and be able to manage complex projects, coordinate multiple activities and tasks, supervise part-time staff and student employees, and assist in the dissemination of the University Archives' electronic records project activities.

In addition, the Electronic Records Archivist will counsel and train administrative and academic units in electronic record-keeping processes and workflow that best meet the unit's business needs and compliant with university, state and federal policy. The Electronic Records Archivist I will also perform regular archival duties, including reference service rotations, departmental service and outreach activities as assigned. The archivist will perform other professional functions as needed.

Requirements: Minimum qualifications are a M.A. in Information Science, Library Science, Archival Science, or related field, and a graduate of an archival education program that meets the guidelines of the Society of American Archivists. In addition, an Archivist I must have one or more years of professional experience. The individual should be familiar with cataloging techniques, MARC, DACS, and EAD. The individual must demonstrate knowledge of the management of electronic records and expertise in working with electronic records. Experience processing archival collections and archival reference services required. The individual must be comfortable working with minimal supervision, have good interpersonal and communication skills, and be an effective contributor to team projects.

Director
University Archives & Historical Collections
Michigan State University
East Lansing, MI

Michigan State University (MSU) seeks a Director of the University Archives & Historical Collections (UAHC), starting January 3, 2008. The UAHC is chartered by the MSU Board of Trustees to act as the institutional memory through the preservation of and access to University historical and business records. In this capacity, UAHC is assuming an increasing leadership role in developing the University's policies and practices for managing digital records and objects. MSU is engaged in a major project to upgrade its enterprise business systems, and UAHC staff are involved, working to ensure that the University's information systems and related business processes provide appropriate records management and archival functionality. The Director will have a unique opportunity to contribute key leadership to a major research university's initiative in emerging methods for electronic records management and archiving.

The UAHC also collects and preserves materials of historical value not directly relating to University history. These materials comprise the Historical Collections and cover areas of local, regional, national and international interest, from the papers of Michigan politicians to the diaries of Civil War soldiers. The UAHC supports the University's missions of teaching, research and public service through outreach and engagement by making its collections available to faculty, student and guest researchers, and by supporting instruction and scholarship in a variety of ways.

The Director of the UAHC reports to the Vice Provost for Libraries, Computing and Technology, who is in the role of the University's CIO. The Director will be responsible for the operations of the UAHC, including obtaining new materials, developing and directing grant proposals, budgeting and budget management, managing the staff, working with development staff to build external support for the UAHC, personal research, and continuing the national and international leadership of the UAHC in the field of records and archival management. The Director will be expected to possess and exercise management competencies facilitating effective collaboration with other University academic and support units in achieving the goals of both the University and the UAHC, as well as effective management of the UAHC and its staff and other resources.

The UAHC holds over 30,000 cubic feet of records, over 1,000 private collections, more than 100,000 photographic images, more than a million photographic negatives, thousands of movie films, videos, and other visual materials. The UAHC maintains an oral history of the University started in 1999. This project continues and has to date conducted over 100 interviews that have been transcribed and indexed.

Digital Records Archivist

The Pennsylvania State University Libraries seek applications and nominations for the position of Digital Records Archivist. The person appointed to this tenure-track, faculty position will manage the Eberly Family Special Collections Library's existing born digital archival holdings and expand its capacity to collect electronic records with the initial effort focused on university records.

The Eberly Family Special Collections Library at University Park comprises three units: Historical Collections and Labor Archives, Rare Books and Manuscripts, and University Archives and Records Management, together including a total of 18 full-time faculty and staff. The University Archives oversees the University Records Management Program and Inactive Records Center, an extensive sports archives, photograph and audio-visual collections, as well as Fred Waring's America. More information about all special collections in the University Libraries is available online at http://www.libraries.psu.edu/psul/speccolls.html.

Responsibilities:
The Digital Records Archivist will help develop and implement workflows and processes enabling the effective acquisition, description, access, management and preservation of a broad range of digital content, including university records, websites, email, and personal digital archives. This position reports to the Head of the Eberly Family Special Collections Library and works closely with the University Archivist, other archival professionals, librarians, information technologists, and records creators throughout the University. The archivist will manage day-to-day activities in conjunction with the development and management of repository services, the web archiving program, and a wide variety of born-digital records ingest and access initiatives. The archivist will take the lead in identifying digital records of continuing institutional value and in developing strategies for long-term preservation and access. The archivist will be expected to remain current with emerging standards and professional best practices and be able to manage complex projects, coordinate multiple activities and tasks, supervise part-time and student employees, and curate electronic records and digital collections throughout the information lifecycle. The archivist will also perform regular archival duties, including reference service and outreach activities, and assist in the dissemination of best practices, trend reports, and operational guidelines. The archivist will perform other professional functions as needed.

Requirements:
Minimum qualifications are a MLS/MLIS from an ALA-accredited program (or equivalent), or a Masters in Information Science, Archival Science, or related field. Experience working with the curation of digital content in an archival repository. Familiarity with descriptive and data structure metadata standards such as MARC, DAS, EAD, Dublin Core, METS, MODS, and PREMIS. Familiarity with tools and workflows being developed to support the ingest and management of born digital records. Demonstrated knowledge of the management, preservation, and access of electronic records, and expertise in working with electronic records. Demonstrated knowledge of data storage methods, media, security, content management, and access. The candidate must have excellent analytical, interpersonal and communication skills, be an effective team contributor, have proven ability to manage projects and competing priorities with demonstrated ability to be flexible, to adapt to change, and to work successfully in a fast-paced, dynamic environment.

Preferred: Experience processing archival collections and providing archival reference services; experience working with tools that verify file authenticity, search for personal identity information, and harvest websites; programming/scripting skills in languages such as Java, PERL, and XSLT.

**WASHINGTON UNIVERSITY
JOB DESCRIPTION**

DATE:

JOB TITLE: Film & Media Digital Archivist
GRADE: 10 **FLSA:**
JOB CODE:

SUPERVISOR: David Rowntree
DEPARTMENT: Film & Media Archive (Special Collections)

****

POSITION SUMMARY:

Washington University Libraries Film & Media Archive seeks an enthusiastic, innovative and technically-oriented colleague to join one of the most dynamic and interesting media archives in the nation. The Digital Archivist will assume management responsibilities of all digital activities and initiatives in the Archive. This individual will coordinate efforts to digitize materials in the collection and develop strategies for long-term preservation of these digital assets. The Archivist will also contribute to the efforts of the Digital Library initiative by working closely with Digital Library Services (DLS) and spearhead efforts to enhance our online resources. The Archivist will work with others within the library system and with faculty to facilitate and increase the use of digital materials from our collections on campus, in research, and in the classroom. The position reports to the Special Media Collections Archivist.

PRIMARY DUTIES AND RESPONSIBILITIES (Essential Functions)

1. Manage the digital assets in the film archive, including digitization, creation of metadata, cataloging, and working with DLS on long-term preservation, storage, and migration of digital materials. (50%)

2. Lead the efforts to increase and maintain a web presence for the archive, including managing the archive website, adding content, editing digital video and audio, and overseeing staff and students involved in these initiatives. (25%)

3. Participate in developing and delivering instructional and outreach programs of the Film and Media Archive; assume a role in digital projects initiated by faculty for classroom development, research, and teaching. (10%)

4. Participate in tasks that will strengthen the operations of the archive including assistance in grant writing, participation in archive and library meetings, patron services, and interactions with faculty. Participates in committee work within Washington University Libraries and completes special projects as assigned. (10%)

5. Remain current with trends and developments in digital formats, preservation, access, and file transfer and management systems. (5%)

MINIMUM EDUCATION/EXPERIENCE: Masters Degree or Graduate Level Certificate

PREFERRED EDUCATION/EXPERIENCE: A Master's degree or Graduate level Certificate in moving image archives, library and information science, film studies or other related degrees. Experience working with audio/video formats and files, digitization of linear media, website development, and editing digital media is required. Experience with editing software on Final Cut Pro is preferred. Previous archival education or experience preferred. Knowledge of African-American history and documentary filmmaking is a benefit. Evidence of written, oral communication and web management skills is required.

CRITICAL SKILLS AND EXPERTISE: Previous archival experience or education required. Knowledge of digital formats and African-American history, film, and documentary filmmaking is a benefit. Evidence of written and oral communication skills required. Experience working with digital video and audio equipment, files and formats, compression codecs, and web delivery is desired.

REQUIRED LICENSURE/CERTIFICATION/REGISTRATION:

DECISION MAKING AND IMPACT:
The position will make regular decisions on materials to be digitized, formats used, and the structure of metadata information gathered for the digital files. There are no concrete standards for digital materials; therefore it will be important for this person to stay abreast of new technologies and emerging practices. Principles guiding these decisions will be determined in collaboration with the supervisor and Digital Library Team. The impact of these decisions will affect the process and workflow for making materials accessible online as well as strategies for long-term digital storage and preservation.

FINANCIAL/OPERATIONAL IMPACT: None

CONTACTS:

Internal – The person will interact mainly with archive staff and Digital Library Services.

External – Most external contact will be with vendors and moving image archivists who also are managing digital content.

SUPERVISION:

Given – None
Received – Employee will often work closely with the supervisor to develop goals and strategies in the archive as it pertains digitization, editing, and preservation.

UNIVERSITY OF WATERLOO
Digital Special Collections Librarian
http://www.hr.uwaterloo.ca/.jd/00001408.html

WATERLOO | HUMAN RESOURCES

Digital Special Collections Librarian

Department:	Library - Special Collections	Effective Date:	January, 2012
Grade:	USG 8-13	Reports to:	Head Special Collections
	35 hr/wk		

General Accountability

This position is accountable to the Head, Special Collections for developing and implementing the Special Collections digital preservation & digitization for preservation program, including policies, workflows and processes for the appraisal, acquisition, description, storage, preservation and discovery of digital special collections and archives.

Working closely with support from, and in collaboration with, Library Systems, IST partners, liaison librarians, content creators and owners and others across the Library, the Digital Special Collections Librarian is responsible to:

- Collaboratively develop and implement the Library's digital preservation & digitization for preservation program, including policies, workflows and processes for the appraisal, acquisition, description, storage, preservation and discovery of University and Library academic and administrative digital assets, collections and archives.
- Work across the Library to ensure appropriate and granular discovery, access and management of Library digital assets
- Work with Library and campus stakeholders to articulate, specify and implement technical approaches and infrastructures for digital content archiving and preservation, recognizing that these may vary with the content and use case
- Perform other advanced archival work, when required, relating to the management of archival records in analogue formats. These responsibilities are carried out in accordance with standards and best practices for digital curation and preservation, archival principles, institutional policies, procedures and priorities.
- Participate in the monitoring and development of national and international standards for digital curation and digital preservation, archives management, and participate in the formulation of local and regional (eg. TUG, OCUL) policies and procedures.
- Participate in the marketing, outreach and education of digital preservation best practices, resources and services across the Library and with the Ontario Council of University Libraries (OCUL) and other regional bodies.

Nature and Scope

UNIVERSITY OF WATERLOO

Digital Special Collections Librarian

http://www.hr.uwaterloo.ca/.jd/00001408.html

This position is one of three reporting to the Head, Special Collections. The others are the Archivist, Special Collections, and the Library Clerk/Secretary. The Doris Lewis Rare Book Room houses literary and historical archive collections serving the research needs of undergraduates, graduates, faculty members, community members and outside researchers. Staff provide reference assistance by mail, telephone, personal visit or electronically. The collections include the University of Waterloo Archives, comprised of official records of University administrative offices, faculties and departments, and materials created by University-related groups and private donors, documenting the history of the University. Access to these materials is provided to the university community and outside researchers in accordance with University of Waterloo policies and guidelines, the Canadian Copyright Act, the Ontario Freedom of Information and Protection of Personal Privacy Act, and, for private donations, the donor's wishes as stated upon transfer of documents.

The incumbent provides leadership with respect to the curation and preservation of born-digital and digitized materials, and the integration of long-term digital preservation services into existing Library services. The incumbent provides support to other Library staff, recognizes and encourages their contributions and builds productive, team-based relationships, and also leads by building effective working relationships with other staff at the University of Waterloo and in other TUG Libraries.

The incumbent develops expertise in emerging national and international standards for digital archives, digital curation and preservation – such as the Open Archival Information System (OAIS) Reference Model, digital preservation metadata standards (e.g., PREMIS, METS), and emerging standards for trusted digital repositories – as well as standards for other archives functions, such as archival description. The incumbent is responsible for the creation and maintenance of internal files which support the provision of discovery and access services, and must also be familiar with other Library policies and procedures.

Increasingly, literary and historical archives and university archives collections include "born-digital" materials or materials requiring digitization for their continuing preservation and access. The incumbent will, starting with University Archives, develop and manage the Library's digitization for preservation and digital repository services, the university web archive, and associated discovery and access initiatives for born-digital and digitized collections. The incumbent will liaise with the university records manager and other university officials, in identifying university digital assets of enduring institutional value, and in developing strategies for their long-term preservation and use.

The incumbent will also work closely with Library departments, providing assistance and guidance to librarians and staff who are creating or have digital assets that are of lasting interest to the University and broader academic disciplinary communities.

Information access management aspects of this position include appraisal, accessioning, arrangement, description and preservation of archival materials, both digital and analogue. For each collection the incumbent creates an accession record and inventory; determines a logical, informative and appropriate arrangement which conforms to archival principles; conducts historical research to determine biographical and historical information relating to the collection; identifies the metadata required to ensure that the content, context, and structure of the collection will continue to be available and understandable to researchers, and that the collection will remain usable; creates a finding aid; and, for digital materials, ensures that copies of digital records and their associated metadata can be made available to all users who require them. The incumbent provides information access to digital and analogue archival materials according to national and international standards as appropriate and as they are evolving. The incumbent is responsible for the establishment, documentation and implementation of processing procedures for digital archives and digital special collections necessary to maintain intellectual and administrative control of the collections.

The public service aspect of this position requires detailed knowledge of the background and content of both book and archival collections in the Department for the provision of information service and the preparation of exhibits and occasional publications, and requires as well knowledge of methods of research. The incumbent acts as liaison between the Library and University Faculties and units and performs research at the request of University officials and administrative departments and must have a broad knowledge of the history of the University and its administrative and academic organization. The incumbent assists as requested in University and Library development activities and related events, performing research and providing materials for anniversaries, open houses, reunions, yearbooks, slide shows, histories and other publications.

The incumbent will lead diverse project teams of individuals working on digital preservation efforts throughout the Library, and may have co-op students, technical staff and assistant archivists reporting to them as required.

Statistical Data

Specific Accountabilities

1. To lead the development and implementation of the Library's digital preservation and digitization program including for example integration with discovery and access of locally managed tools.
2. To manage digital collections and archives of textual, graphic, audio-visual, research data and other materials by accessioning, arranging, describing, preserving, and making them available for use, through the associated OAIS functions of ingest, archival storage, administration, access, and preservation planning.
3. To maintain an awareness of national and international standards and practices including those emerging and under development, recommending these for local use.
4. To assist with the management of collections in analogue formats by accessioning, arranging, describing, preserving, and making them available for use.
5. To articulate, create and maintain internal and external electronic records, documents, indexes and files which facilitate processing, information access management and reference/research functions.
6. To provide information access to archival collections in accordance with international and national standards, with the Department's policies, needs (including requirements for monetary appraisal), standards and to maintain related files.
7. To ensure the continued development of existing special collections by assisting with the appraisal and acquisitions function, particularly regarding transfers of digital archives and collections.
8. To perform research as appropriate and to provide information service to researchers by answering specific reference requests concerning the collections, invigilating researchers using the collections, providing assistance to users, and preparing displays, presentations and by preparing and updating electronic publications, finding aids and guides.
9. To supervise part-time activity in the preparation of materials for archives.
10. To lead or participate in the planning and execution of special projects and to participate on task groups or committees when required.

Digital Archivist

Manuscripts & Archives

Sterling Memorial Library

Yale University

Rank: Librarian II

The University and the Library

The Yale University Library, as one of the world's leading research libraries, collects, organizes, preserves, and provides access to and services for a rich and unique record of human thought and creativity. It fosters intellectual growth and supports the teaching and research missions of Yale University and scholarly communities worldwide. A distinctive strength is its rich spectrum of resources, including approximately thirteen million volumes and information in all media, ranging from ancient papyri to early printed books to electronic databases. The Library is engaging in numerous projects to expand access to its physical and digital collections. Housed in twenty-two buildings including the Sterling Memorial Library, the Beinecke Rare Book and Manuscript Library, and the new Bass Library, it employs a dynamic and diverse staff of nearly six hundred who offer innovative and flexible services to library readers. For additional information on the Yale University Library, please visit the Library's Web site at: www.library.yale.edu.

General Purpose

Reporting to the Senior Archivist for Digital Information Systems/Head of the University Archives, the Digital Archivist will join a dynamic group of archivists and helps to ensure effective acquisition, description, preservation, future migration, access to and security of digital component of manuscripts collections acquired by the department. Primary focus will be on the management, appraisal, description, and preservation of born-digital components of manuscripts collections.

Responsibilities

Drives management, appraisal, description, and preservation of born-digital components of manuscripts collections. Explores and proposes new technologies, including Web 2.0, to meet research and reference needs of patrons and staff. Serves as the systems team liaison to the public services unit. Under the direction of the Senior Archivist for Digital

Information Services, the systems team employs digital technologies to transform departmental processes and operations and ensures the functioning of the department's technology infrastructure. Serves as the web manager for the Manuscripts & Archives and Fortunoff Video Archive for Holocaust Testimonials (VAHT) public web portals, utilizing Cascade Server content management system, and is responsible for maintaining and updating the department's internal policies and procedures web site, utilizing SharePoint. Assists in research services functions of the department through weekly service on the reference desk, involvement in primary source instruction, and assistance with the exhibit program. Utilizing departmental and library digital infrastructure, manages preservation and access copies resulting from digital duplication. Assesses existing infrastructure and suggests changes as necessary. Supports and manages technical aspects of the VAHT digitization collections digitization project. Actively participates in library- and university-wide efforts to preserve and disseminate digital collections, wherever that work might be undertaken. Serves on requisite committees, as necessary. In particular, participates in the development of digital repository functionality to support users in determining the existence, description, location, and availability of digital collections stored in the repository, as well as applying restrictions and controls to limit access to specially protected collections, generating responses, and delivering the responses to users. Addresses the integration of digital collections with EAD finding aids. Provides technical skills (XML, XSL – stylesheet transformation and XSL FO for PDF generation) to support EAD finding aids maintenance and development throughout the Yale University Library. Engages actively with professional organizations and literature; keeps abreast of archival trends and developments. Participates in and contributes to library long-term planning and is professionally active in library, scholarly and/or academic organizations. Represents the library and the University in the academic and professional community by serving on various committees and task forces. May be required to assist with disaster recovery efforts. May be assigned to work at West Campus location in West Haven, CT.

Qualifications

Master's degree from an ALA-accredited program for library and information science and/or Master's degree in history or related discipline; and a minimum of two years professional archival or digital records management experience and demonstrated professional accomplishments. Demonstrated knowledge of digital archival and records management principles and practices, as well as the systems and automation techniques utilized. Demonstrated ability to work with databases, migrate data from one database system to another, and develop functional requirements for programmers building new database applications. Familiarity with EAD, MODS, METS, XML/XSL and other data structure standards relevant to the archival control of digital collection materials.

Demonstrated ability to communicate effectively, both orally and in writing. Demonstrated skills in web site creation and management. Ability to work independently and collaboratively in a team environment. **Preferred**: Experience integrating digital and non-digital material into archival arrangement and description. Experience with web-based content management systems and page authoring tools such as Cascade Server and SharePoint. Experience providing reference service in an academic repository. Ability to conduct training in technical areas.

Head of Digital Information Systems and the University Archives
Manuscripts & Archives
Sterling Memorial Library
Yale University
Rank: Librarian III-V

The University and the Library

The Yale University Library, as one of the world's leading research libraries, collects, organizes, preserves, and provides access to and services for a rich and unique record of human thought and creativity. It fosters intellectual growth and supports the teaching and research missions of Yale University and scholarly communities worldwide. A distinctive strength is its rich spectrum of resources, including approximately thirteen million volumes and information in all media, ranging from ancient papyri to early printed books to electronic databases. The Library is engaging in numerous projects to expand access to its physical and digital collections. Housed in twenty-two buildings including the Sterling Memorial Library, the Beinecke Rare Book and Manuscript Library, and the new Bass Library, it employs a dynamic and diverse staff of nearly six hundred who offer innovative and flexible services to library readers. For additional information on the Yale University Library, please visit the Library's Web site at:
www.library.yale.edu.

General Purpose

Reporting to the Director, and supervising the Digital Archivist and Records Services Archivist, the incumbent is responsible for the planning, design, implementation, and maintenance of the department's digital management and descriptive information systems, including systems for the creation, maintenance, and delivery of original and surrogate digital resources. The incumbent plans and supervises user and systems support activities for the department. The incumbent directs the work of the University Archives.

Responsibilities

1. Coordinates systems and digital resources planning in Manuscripts and Archives taking into account professional and industry trends and projections as well as university, library, and departmental plans. Keeps abreast of professional and technological developments affecting the department's automated systems and digital resources and recommends upgrades, software and equipment purchases, and migration strategies, consistent with university and library objectives and policies.

2. Communicates and coordinates systems and digital resources plans with appropriate professional, university, and library groups through reports, service on committees and active professional contacts. Serves as technical liaison with the Information Technology Office,

Library Access Integration Services, and the university's Technology Services department for systems, electronic records, data warehousing, and related issues.

3. Develops resources needed to advance priority systems and digital resources programs and projects in Manuscripts and Archives through internal budget and resource planning and grant and development proposals.

4. Provides technical and project management leadership and coordination for systems and digital resources development, implementation, and maintenance projects.

5. Directs the department's systems and user support activities to ensure that systems and applications are reliable and that staff are fully trained in their use. Coordinates the use of library and other external systems.

6. Recommends the selection and coordinates the work of outside vendors hired for systems and digital resources projects.

7. Directs strategic planning for the University Archives. Establishes policies and procedures for day-to-day operations, including accessioning, office of origin requests, and backlog processing. Serves as one of the main points of contact with the Secretary of the University, General Counsel for the University, and the Vice President for Finance and Administration.

7. Participates in departmental strategic and action planning, and in the formulation of departmental policies and procedures by assembling information, drafting policy and procedure memoranda, and making recommendations on proposed policies and procedures.

8. Makes recommendations on personal selection, staffing requirements, and equipment and supply needs.

9. Participates in library planning activities and is active professionally.

10. May be required to assist with disaster recovery efforts. May be assigned to work at West Campus location in West Haven, CT.

Qualifications

Required: MA degree in history, computer science, or related discipline and/or ALA accredited MLS. Formal archival and records management, library science, computer science, or related training or education. Five years experience in an archival, records management, library, or similar environment with increasing responsibility for systems development, implementation, or maintenance, including two years experience in a university archives setting. Experience with EAD, MODS, METS, XML/XSL and other data structure standards relevant to the archival control of digital collection materials. Experience with relational database systems, preferably

SQL Server or Access. Experience delivering content in web-based applications. Knowledge of data storage methods, media and security. Excellent oral and written communication skills. Demonstrated ability to work effectively in a team setting with administrative, professional and support staff. Supervisory experience. Demonstrated professional contributions at the regional, national, and/or international level through published writings, conference presentations, professional organization committee/task force work, and/or workshop development and teaching.

Preferred: Professional archival, library, or systems experience in an academic or research library setting. Reference, arrangement and description, or collection development experience in an archival setting. Experience in the development and management of grant-funded projects. Training in project management tools and techniques, such as Microsoft Sharepoint/Project.

ARCHIVIST, DIGITAL PROJECTS & OUTREACH

York University Libraries invite applications for the position of Archivist with the Clara Thomas Archives & Special Collections. The successful candidate will be responsible for the stewardship of digital assets including the management of born-digital records and the creation of digital collections from analog documents (such as sound and moving image recordings, photographs and textual materials), as well as processing records in a wide variety of other media. This is a tenure-track position for an archivist with up to three years of post-graduate experience.

York University offers a world-class, modern, interdisciplinary academic experience in Toronto, Canada's most multicultural city. York is at the centre of innovation, with a thriving community of almost 60,000 faculty, staff and students who challenge the ordinary and deliver the unexpected. The Clara Thomas Archives & Special Collections is a department of York University Libraries holding over 700 metres of university records; over 2,400 metres of private and institutional papers and an extensive collection of non-textual materials. Special Collections has over 20,000 volumes of published Canadiana, including Canadian pamphlets. Additional information on holdings and services can be found at: http://www.library.yorku.ca/ccm/ArchivesSpecialCollections/index.htm

Responsibilities:
The Archivist works within a collaborative and team environment. The incumbent will be an enthusiastic and innovative individual who demonstrates leadership in the creation, development, maintenance and support of digital archival holdings. He/she will work closely with the Digital Initiatives Librarian to develop and implement policies and procedures for the capture, storage and long-term accessibility of these holdings. Working with the Web Librarian, the successful candidate will provide leadership in the development, management and maintenance of the departmental web presence. He/she will show leadership in the development and implementation of a communications/outreach plan for the Clara Thomas Archives and Special Collections. Assists the Head with securing grants and other funding to support digital projects. He/she will be regularly involved in the provision of reference and research services as well as in the appraisal, acquisition, arrangement, RAD-based description, and physical processing of private papers and university records. Will participate in instruction of undergraduate and graduate students in the use of archival holdings. The incumbent will be committed to scholarship, professional development and service.

Qualifications:
- Master's in archival studies from a graduate programme conforming to the Association of Canadian Archivists' Guidelines for the Development of a Two-Year Curriculum for a Master's of Archival Studies, or MLS (or equivalent) with concentration in professional archival education
- Up to three years of professional archival experience in an established archive, preferably in an academic setting
- Demonstrated experience in using computer applications for the management of archival holdings and the creation of digital documents for outreach via virtual exhibits, blogs etc.
- Awareness of funding opportunities and of the grant-writing process
- Demonstrated experience in the creation of promotional materials for cultural programming (preferably archives)
- Demonstrated knowledge of media conversion technologies
- Demonstrated knowledge of the creation and management of electronic records
- Demonstrated project management skills
- Excellent oral and written communication and instruction skills
- Excellent organizational, analytical and interpersonal skills
- Ability to work independently and in collaboration with others
- Ability to manage a complex workload in a timely, effective manner with minimum supervision
- In-depth knowledge of current trends and issues in archives, including RAD and EAD

Digital Assets Librarian, York University Libraries

York University Libraries are seeking an innovative and self-motivated individual for the position of Digital Assets Librarian in Bibliographic Services.

York University is the leading interdisciplinary research and teaching university in Canada. York offers a modern, academic experience at the undergraduate and graduate level in Toronto, Canada's most international city. The third largest university in the country, York is host to a dynamic academic community of 62,000 students, faculty and staff, as well as 240,000 alumni worldwide. York's 10 Faculties and 28 research centres conduct ambitious, groundbreaking research that is interdisciplinary, cutting across traditional academic boundaries.

The Digital Assets Librarian will join a dynamic and growing team at York University Libraries, actively participating in research on campus, OCUL-Scholars Portal programs, and national and international digital initiatives. Working collaboratively in a dynamic service-oriented environment, the Digital Assets Librarian will play an integral role in the development of data curation, asset management and preservation strategies for York University Libraries. He/she will enable data discovery and retrieval, preserve and maintain data quality, provide for data re-use over time, and develop other value-added services.

The successful candidate will have a proven track record of managing large-scale projects involving stakeholders spanning multiple areas. The incumbent will ensure that best practices in emerging metadata standards are established and followed. This position will perform a key role in the creation of new data repository tools by gathering requirements and coordinating software development projects. He/she will play an advocacy and promotion role for open access to research data, best practices in data curation, and preservation practices on campus. The Digital Assets Librarian will work closely with colleagues, faculty, and staff to provide a wide range of curatorial services, including consulting on best practices for data documentation, developing appropriate data management plans, and coordinating the receipt of new data acquisitions. The Digital Assets Librarian responsibilities will include a liaison assignment with an academic department.

Additionally, the incumbent will possess: an enthusiastic and flexible attitude; the capacity to adapt to a changing environment; the ability to balance multiple responsibilities; demonstrated time management skills; and knowledge of emerging trends in scholarly communications and library and information technologies.

Qualifications:
- MLS degree (or recognized equivalent) from an ALA-accredited program;
- demonstrated large-scale project management expertise;
- demonstrated experience with XML, applying metadata standards and schema, and controlled vocabularies;
- demonstrated expertise with one or more metadata manipulation and scripting languages (e.g. XSLT, Perl, Python);
- demonstrated applied web application development experience, including familiarity with development frameworks (e.g. Ruby on Rails, Django), and application programming language(s) such as Java, PHP, or others;
- familiarity with semantic and linked data standards such as RDF and OWL;

- familiarity with standards and best practices in data curation and preservation;
- strong understanding of emerging trends and issues for research libraries in the areas of digital curation, digital preservation, scholarly communications and metadata;
- excellent independent learning and problem-solving abilities;
- excellent oral and written communication skills, ability to work independently and in collaboration with others;
- evidence of a developing research portfolio

This is a continuing-stream (tenure track) appointment to be filled at the Assistant Librarian level and appropriate for a librarian with up to nine years of post-MLS experience. Librarians and archivists at York University have academic status and are members of the York University Faculty Association bargaining unit (http://www.yufa.org/). Salary is commensurate with qualifications. The position is available from June 1, 2012. All York University positions are subject to budgetary approval.

York University is an Affirmative Action Employer. The Affirmative Action Program can be found on York's website at www.yorku.ca/acadjobs or a copy can be obtained by calling the affirmative action office at 416-736-5713. All qualified candidates are encouraged to apply; however, Canadian citizens and Permanent Residents will be given priority.

Collection Policies

http://bentley.umich.edu   bhlwebarchive@umich.edu   (734)764-3482   1150 Beal Ave. Ann Arbor, MI 48109

Bentley Historical Library Web Archives:
Collection Development Policy
Nancy Deromedi and Michael Shallcross
Digital Curation

Version 2.0 (August 2, 2011)

Table of Contents

1

Collection Development Policies

The Bentley Historical Library has articulated collection development policies for both UARP and MHC that govern the identification, appraisal, and selection of content for the respective web archives of each division. These policies are informed by the library's main collecting priorities, archival principles, professional best practices, and analyses of manuscript collections and record groups.

The Bentley Historical Library is mindful of the widespread use and significance of social media and Web 2.0 technologies at the University of Michigan and across the state. Archivists have been unable to preserve social media websites (as of August 2011) due to various technical difficulties. In addition to the challenges posed by the structure and design of social media sites, robots.txt exclusions have severely restricted the library's ability to archive such resources. Moving forward, archivists will work with content owners and the California Digital Library to develop interim solutions and also monitor the work of the International Internet Preservation Consortium (IIPC) to preserve social media sites more effectively.

University Archives and Records Program

The collection development policy for the University of Michigan Web Archives is based upon UARP's *Records Policy and Procedures Manual*, the University of Michigan Standard Practice Guide 601.08, and the mandate set forth in Section 12.04 of the Board of Regents Bylaws.

Selection Criteria

For inclusion in the University of Michigan Web Archives, a website must meet the following criteria:

- The website falls within UARP's collecting scope as it is established by the *Records Policy and Procedures Manual*. It should be created, owned, or used by university units, faculty, or students in carrying out university-related business or functions. This guideline excludes web pages about—but not *by*—the university (such as online articles in *The Chronicle of Higher Education*).

- The website complements or has related material among manuscript collections and record groups. UARP seeks to expand upon existing holdings or develop areas that have been previously under-documented.

- The informational/evidential value of the website is made clear in its representation of administration, instruction, research, creative work, competitions, or social events at the University of Michigan. The website should contain meaningful content and adequately illustrate or promote understanding of its subject matter.

August 2, 2011   9

- The website and the content therein are unique.

- The website is not merely transactional or related to the delivery of routine products or services.

- The website reflects basic functions or activities associated with colleges and universities: administration, teaching, research, service, student life, and athletic competitions.

To ensure that its policy remains flexible, UARP has identified several exceptions to the above criteria. On a case-by-case basis, archivists may consider websites related to alumni or organizations, individuals, and events affiliated with (but not part of) the university. Archivists may also select a wider range of content in case of important events, breaking news, or upon special request by university units.

Collecting Priorities

The _Records Policy and Procedures Manual_ outlines UARP's basic collecting priorities. In developing the University of Michigan Web Archives, UARP has followed these priorities in an initial two-phase process of systematic website preservation. In addition to the ongoing maintenance of existing collections and selection of newly released content, archivists may launch additional phases in response to new projects or initiatives within UARP or developments in the university's online presence.

Phase 1: July 2010 – February 2011
In this phase, UARP initially focused on its highest collecting priority: administrative and academic units, a category that includes all major administrative offices as well as the 19 schools and colleges of the main campus. Sites related to these units were analyzed for the inclusion of content related to research, instruction, and creative work within the schools and colleges. Particular emphasis was placed on collecting web pages related to faculty members from the School of Art + Design and the School of Music, Theatre & Dance, since these individuals and units have been under-documented in existing record groups and collections. This phase also involved preserving websites related to the university's centers and institutes, museums and libraries, and athletic department.

Phase 2: February 2011 -
The second phase of UARP's collection development for the University of Michigan Web Archives involves the broader selection of websites related to prominent faculty members, research projects, and student organizations. Special mention needs to be made in regards to the appraisal and preservation of faculty and student organization websites. In addition to the above-mentioned criteria, the selection of faculty member websites will depend upon:
- The faculty member's prior selection for inclusion in the University Archives.
- The faculty member's professional stature, awards, and recognition (including named chairs).

August 2, 2011

10

- Use patterns and frequency of updates for the site in question.

Archivists conducted a survey of student organization websites in 2010 and will use this information as a basis for preservation decisions. The selection of student organization sites will involve this information as well as a consideration of the following guidelines:

- The organization's prior selection for inclusion in the University Archives.
- The stature, history, and organizational viability of the group.
- Use patterns and frequency of updates for the site in question.

The preliminary survey suggested that student groups are using Facebook and Twitter more frequently than traditional websites; UARP may therefore explore the preservation of such content in the future.

Ongoing Activities (as of 2011):
Collection development for the University of Michigan Web Archives will involve the active maintenance and upkeep of archived content and the identification, appraisal, and selection of newly released content in accordance with the above-mentioned priorities. Archivists will evaluate captures and remove content that has significant technical issues and may revisit earlier appraisal decisions if the archived version of a website is missing significant content. Archivists will also review websites of the highest priority groups to ensure that they have not undergone significant changes that could impact preservation (such as changed host names/URLs). This ongoing work will require archivists to stay abreast of news reports and maintain relationships with unit webmasters to be aware of significant changes to or new releases of high-profile sites.

Michigan Historical Collections
The collections development policy for the Michigan Historical Collections Web Archives is based upon the mandate set forth in Section 12.04 of the Board of Regents Bylaws and MHC's existing collecting priorities.

Selection Criteria
Since 1986 the Michigan Historical Collections has used a process of collecting priorities to guide its acquisition of archives and manuscript collections. In selecting websites for permanent preservation, we work within our highest topical priorities, and follow these selection criteria:

- Websites of organizations and persons whose archives we are committed to preserve.

- Websites of other organizations and persons to fill gaps in our collections.

August 2, 2011

11

- Websites that are well developed with rich content documenting the work and thought of the person or organization.

- Websites that periodically incorporate new content.

- Websites with content that is not likely to be duplicated in an individual or organization's paper records.

Collecting Priorities

Based on the library's mission as established by the University of Michigan Board of Regents to document "the state, its institutions, and its social, economic, and intellectual development" and the historical collecting patterns of the library, the MHC developed a list of 19 topical collecting areas: Agriculture, Commerce and Industry, Communications, Creative Expression, Education, Ethnicity, Family, Gender and Sexuality, Labor, Leisure, Military, Natural Resources, Pioneer Michigan, Politics and public policy, Professionals, Recreation, Religion, Science and Technology, and Transportation.

Within these 21 areas, and working to document the entire state of Michigan, a set of priorities has been developed and is periodically reviewed and adjusted. The process of setting collecting priorities is described by Christine Weideman's "A New Map for Field Work: Impact of Collections Analysis on the Bentley Historical Library"[2] and Judith E. Endelman's "Looking Backward to Plan for the Future: Collection Analysis for Manuscript Repositories."[3]

---

[2] *American Archivist,* Winter 1991, Vol. 54, Issue 1, pp. 54-60.
[3] *American Archivist,* Summer 1987, Vol. 50, Issue 3, pp. 340-355.

August 2, 2011

12

Michigan State University Archives and Historical Collections
Collection Policy   Draft: September 16, 2009

Mission

Michigan State University Archives and Historical Collections provides records management services to the university and preserves and provides access to the institution's historical records. The University Archives also maintains historical collections that support faculty and student research and classroom instruction.

Mandate

The mandate of the Michigan State University Archives and Historical Collections is founded on a resolution of the Board of Trustees, as recorded in the minutes of November 21, 1969. This resolution claimed all records of the official activities of university officers and offices as the property of Michigan State University, and that such property could not be destroyed without the approval of the Director of Archives. The full name, "University Archives and Historical Collections," was established during a meeting of the Board of Trustees, as recorded in the minutes of September 17, 1970, to reflect the Archives' identity as a repository for historically significant collections as well as university records.

Audience

As the official repository of Michigan State University's permanent records, the Archives serves the entire University community including its administration, faculty, staff and students. The Archives supports and encourages new research by scholars from MSU and from other institutions. The Archives also provides guidance and services in records management to the University's academic and administrative units.

The staff welcome inquiries from public and local historians; publishers and producers; K-12 students, teachers, genealogists, and the general public.

University Archives

Michigan State University, the nation's first land-grant college, has been a leader in scholarship and research in fields as diverse as agriculture, medicine, law-enforcement, and nuclear science. The University established an international presence in the course of the twentieth century, and has brought its land-grant heritage and mission to Japan, Rwanda, Vietnam, Dubai, and other locations around the globe. Closer to home, the university has partnered with state and local agencies, farmers, and scholars for the benefit of social, scientific and agricultural concerns throughout the state of Michigan and the Great Lakes region.

The Archives is the official and foremost repository for records pertaining to the history of Michigan State University. The university collections are particularly strong in regard to the official records of the Board of Trustees; the Presidents and Provosts; the physical campus and grounds; student life (especially the early years of MSU); and publications both by and about students and faculty. Highlights of the collections include the nation-building "Vietnam Project" of 1954-1961; records of MSU's state cooperative extensions; film and video recordings of university sports from the 1950s to the 1970s; and the papers of university president John Hannah; botanist William J. Beal; chemist and politician Robert C. Kedzie; and forensic scientist Ralph Turner.

Records Management

The MSU Archives is responsible for the management of the university's inactive records, including administrative records, publications, and the papers of university faculty, staff, students, and alumni. The MSU Archives assists university units in the efficient administration and management of official paper and electronic records (active and inactive) of the university. The Archives staff also provides ongoing support and training to the university community in records management, storage, and retrieval in order to ensure compliance with all relevant state and federal laws and regulations.

Historical Collections

The MSU Archives also houses collections about history, culture, nature, and life in the state of Michigan and the Great Lakes region. Among these historical collections are administrative and photographic records of the 4-H club in Michigan; the papers of Ransom E. Olds and the REO Motor Car Company; over one hundred Civil War collections concerning natives of Michigan; and the records of several prominent Michigan lumber companies. The Archives' materials are particularly strong for the community of East Lansing, including a large photograph collection, scrapbooks, diaries, and records of local organizations such as the East Lansing Planning Commission.

The Archives has an active interest in records pertaining to the state of Michigan and the Great Lakes region, with particular emphasis on materials that complement existing collections or have a relation of some kind to the university and its research specialties.

Opportunities

In addition to the topics mentioned above, the MSU Archives is intent on building its collections regarding the research, preservation and use of Michigan's environment and the development of alternative energy sources throughout the state. Areas of interest related to this focus include climate change; environmental stewardship (including operations and packaging on campus); bio-energy and alternative fuels; aquaculture; and water and land resource management. The Archives has a particular interest in research conducted by MSU faculty in fields such as economics, nuclear physics, bio-technologies, food sciences, human medicine, and genome-based studies for health and agriculture.

The MSU Archives also seeks faculty papers and research that would expand the representation of female and minority faculty in the collections and which document significant research and pedagogical achievements. University athletics, both intercollegiate and intramural, is another priority for the Archives, as is the student experience at MSU during the late twentieth and early twenty-first centuries. A valuable component of this focus includes records of student organizations, such as service groups; professional societies; special interest clubs; fraternities and sororities; and cultural and religious groups.

In the future, the Archives will strive to identify and collect material related to areas of interest to Michigan State University and its student and faculty communities.

S:\Policies and Procedures\Collection Policy\UAHC_collection_policy_16 Sept 09.docx

Gift/Purchase Agreements

David M. Rubenstein Rare Book & Manuscript Library
Duke University

Electronic Records Addendum

The Donor acknowledges that the Library acquires the materials with the intent of making them available for an ongoing or indefinite period of time. In order to accomplish this, the Library may need to transfer some or all of these materials from the original media as supplied by the donor to new forms of media to ensure their ongoing availability and preservation. The donor grants the library rights to make preservation and access copies of materials in the collection and to make those copies available for use.

The Library may contract with university staff or outside contractors to store, evaluate, manage and or analyze materials in the collection. Any such arrangements must abide by the terms of this agreement.

Upon accessioning, the Library will transfer all electronic records to a secure server space with restricted access. Descriptions created for each group of records will indicate whether or not they are likely to contain Secure Electronic Information (SEI). When the records are processed, the Library will use standard software packages to scan the content for common types of SEI (phone numbers, social security numbers, etc.) Records containing SEI will be embargoed and processed later in accordance with any restrictions outlined in this agreement and with the Library's policies and practices.

Does the Library have your permission to decrypt passwords or encryption systems, if any, to gain access to electronic data received as part of the materials?
_____ Yes
_____ No
If no, such materials may not be retained by the Library.

Does the Library have your permission to recover deleted files or file fragments, if any, and provide access to them to researchers?
___ Yes
___ Yes, under the following conditions
___ No

Does the Library have your permission to preserve and provide access to log files, system files, and other similar data that document your use of computers or systems, if any are received with the materials?
___ Yes
___ Yes, under the following conditions
___ No

Privacy

The Library will review the materials in the collection in an attempt to identify items that contain sensitive information. Please indicate below your awareness of materials that may sensitive information.

___To the best of my knowledge, these materials do not contain sensitive information.

OR

___I believe that the materials are likely to contain sensitive information such as
____Social Security numbers
____Bank account numbers

_____Passwords
_____Medical records
_____Counseling records
_____Student records
_____Employment records
_____Materials covered by attorney-client privilege
_____Research data related to human subjects
_____Federally Classified or Federally restricted materials
_____Other materials that have specific privacy concerns, please specify_____

Records Policy and Procedures Manual: Access Policies

Home   Exhibits   Reference   University Records   Michigan History   Digital Curation   Search

Home > University Archives > Manual

TABLE OF CONTENTS

Section 3: Access Policies

University records are public records and once fully processed are generally open to research use. Records that contain personally identifiable information will be restricted in order to protect individual privacy. Certain administrative records are restricted in accordance with university policy as outlined below. The restriction of university records is subject to compliance with applicable laws, including the Freedom of Information Act (FOIA).

CATEGORIES OF RESTRICTED RECORDS

- Personnel related records, including search, review, promotion, and tenure files, are restricted for thirty years from date of creation.
- Student educational records are restricted for seventy-five years from date of creation.
- Patient/client records are restricted for one-hundred years from date of creation.
- Executive Officers, Deans and Directors records
  As of January 1, 2001, university records generated by the university's Executive Officers, Deans, Directors and their support offices are restricted for a period of twenty years from their date of accession by the Bentley Historical Library. The restriction is subject to applicable law, most notably the Freedom of Information Act (FOIA).

For further information on the restriction policy and placing FOIA requests for restricted material, consult the reference archivist at the Bentley Historical Library or the University of Michigan Freedom of Information Office website

UARP Records Policy and Procedures Manual - January 1993, 1st ed., September 2002, 2nd ed.

1150 Beal Avenue Ann Arbor, MI 48109-2113 U.S.A. | 734.764.3482 | Fax: 734.936.1333
Reference: bentley.ref@umich.edu | Webmaster: bhlwebmaster@umich.edu
Copyright ©2012 The Regents of the University of Michigan
Last modified: July 05, 2007 4:56:05 PM EDT.
Banner image from Jasper Cropsey's The University of Michigan Campus, 1855

http://www.bentley.umich.edu/uarphome/manual/access.php[8/9/12 6:19:34 PM]

DRAFT – July 2011
nancy.kuhl@yale.edu

BEINECKE RARE BOOK & MANUSCRIPT LIBRARY

BORN DIGITAL ARCHIVAL ACQUISITION
COLLECTION & ACCESSION GUIDELINES

The Beinecke Library (BRBL) is committed to collecting, preserving, and providing access to important literary archives including materials documenting creative processes, writing lives, aesthetic communities, publication records, etc. in a range of formats and media. In keeping with this commitment, the Library recognizes and appreciates the increasing and inevitable significance of born-digital materials in literary archives. We have established, therefore, a flexible framework for working with archive creators and their representatives in various contexts to systematically, efficiently, and safely work with born digital manuscripts, correspondence, and related materials as they are acquired, accessioned, organized, maintained, accessed, and used for various research and education purposes.

To that end, the Beinecke Library employs the following guidelines in approaching the assessment, evaluation, collection, capture, accession, and preservation of materials created using digital media;

--BRBL collects digital archival materials in any and all relevant formats (including text, image, sound, etc);

--In acquiring born digital materials, a forensic approach, including the capture by "snapshot" of all working files on a specific computer, will be the preferred method of acquisition; in most cases BRBL will wish to capture entire digital environments without any advanced collection editing by creator or curator;

--Because BRBL is interested in collecting digital materials that have substantive research value, such materials may be segregated from other materials in a broadly-conceived digital archive (spam and other commercial email, for example, may be excluded; extensive personal image or sound file collections may be curated by BRBL before collection and accession). This more limited acquisitions approach will be applied primarily in cases where a small group of materials are to be acquired (a specific body of correspondence, for instance) and not in the case of acquisition of a complete archive;

--In order to retain whatever organization, file structures, and associated data exists in the a digital archive or collection, BRBL staff members need direct access to digital files in their original environment to perform data appraisal, capture, and verification; it is suggested that representatives of archive creators (family and friends, book dealers, agents) should not manipulate, rearrange, extract, copy etc. data from its original source in anticipation of offering the materials to BRBL for gift or purchase.

Beinecke Deed of Gift section applying to curation of born-digital material

6. Terms and Conditions

Yale has accepted Donor's gift of the Property, subject to the following terms and conditions:

B. Donor acknowledges and agrees that upon execution of this Deed of Gift, the Property shall irrevocably become the property of Yale. Donor further acknowledges and agrees that the administration, use, physical display, care, treatment, preservation, conversation, and/or maintenance of the Property, including without limitation any conversion or transferral of the Property into microform, digital format, or any other format or medium now existing or hereinafter devised, shall be at Yale's sole discretion, unless otherwise provided for in this agreement.

Format Policies

SMARTech Help

SMARTech

SMARTech, or Scholarly Materials And Research @ Georgia Tech, is a repository for the capture of the intellectual output of the Institute in support of its teaching and research missions. SMARTech connects stockpiles of digital materials currently in existence throughout campus to create a cohesive, useful, sustainable repository available to Georgia Tech and the world.

See the Mission and Collection Policy .

Why should I participate?

- Access barriers disappear
- Enhanced visibility, use, reputation
- Wide and rapid dissemination of intellectual output
- Supports classroom teaching
- Aids multidisciplinary inquiry
- Valuable recruiting tool
- Preservation and management of information assets
- Reduces duplication of effort
- Stimulates serendipitous discovery and collaboration

What types of materials can I submit and find in SMARTech?

SMARTech houses Georgia Tech research in digital format, including

- Annual Reports
- Conference Papers
- Electronic Theses & Dissertations
- Learning Objects
- Newsletters
- Pre-Prints/Post-Prints
- Proceedings
- Research Reports
- Simulations
- Technical Reports
- Web Pages
- White papers
- Working Papers

What file formats are accepted?

We accept standard formats that we can make a commitment to migrate and provide access to over the long term including:

Type	Description	File extension	Support level
Text/Images	Adobe PDF	pdf	supported
Text	HTML	htm, html	supported
Text	Rich Text Format	rtf	supported
Text	Text	txt	supported
Text	XML	xml	supported
Text	Microsoft Word	doc	known
Text	WordPerfect	wpd	known
Text	SGML	sgm, sgml	known

SMARTech Help

Images	JPEG	jpg, jpeg	supported
Images	GIF	gif	supported
Images	PNG	png	supported
Images	TIFF	tif, tiff	supported
Images	Post Script	ps, eps, ai	supported
Images	BMP	bmp	known
Images	Adobe Photoshop	pdd, psd	known
Images	Microsoft Powerpoint	ppt	known
Images	Photo CD	pcd	known
Video	MPEG	mpg, mpeg, mpe	supported
Video	Video Quicktime	mov, qt	known
Audio	WAV	wav	supported
Audio	MPEG	mpa, abs, mpeg	supported
Audio	AIFF	aiff, aif, aifc	supported
Audio	RealAudio	ra, ram	known
Audio	Basic	au, snd	known
Special	Microsoft Excel	xls	known
Special	Microsoft Project	mpp, mpx, mpd	known
Special	Microsoft Visio	vsd	known
Special	FileMaker/FMP3	fm	known
Special	LateX	latex	known
Special	Mathematica	ma	known
Special	Tex	tex	known
Special	TeXdvi	dvi	known

supported Items in this category can be used in the future through migration or emulation and the Library makes a commitment to do so.

known This category indicates that the specifics of the program code for that format are not public but the format is so widely used that the ability to use it in the future is almost certain.

How are materials in SMARTech preserved?

SMARTech is part of the MetaArchive Cooperative distributed digital preservation network. Georgia Tech Library participates in the MetaArchive program, an international effort for the preservation of electronic scholarly materials through the Library of Congress' National Digital Information Infrastructure and Preservation Program (NDIIPP).

How do I start contributing to SMARTech?

- **email:** smartech@library.gatech.edu

Bentley Historical Library
Digital Curation Services
1150 Beal Avenue
Ann Arbor, MI 48109

Sustainable Formats and Conversion Strategies at the Bentley Historical Library

November 9, 2011
Version 1.0

Executive Summary

The Bentley Historical Library is committed to the long-term preservation of and access to its digital collections. Because the library must contend with thousands of potential file formats, Digital Curation Services has adopted a three-tier approach to facilitate the preservation and conversion of digital content:

- Tier 1: Materials produced in sustainable formats will be maintained in their original version.

- Tier 2: Common "at-risk" formats will be converted to preservation-quality file types to retain important features and functionalities.

- Tier 3: All other content will receive basic bit-level preservation.

This document provides further information on the Bentley Historical Library's accepted preservation formats and conversion strategies.

Please see the chart on pp. 3-5 for a list of sustainable preservation formats and at-risk formats that will be subject to conversion.

Tier 1: Preservation of Sustainable Formats

The library has identified a number of sustainable file formats (pp. 3-5) that are widely used and/or nonproprietary, many of which have been recognized as international standards by bodies such as the International Standards Organization (ISO), ECMA International, and the Organization for the Advancement of Structured Information Standards (OASIS). The longevity of these formats has furthermore been acknowledged by various peer institutions and experts in the digital curation community, including the Library of Congress's National Digital Information Infrastructure and Preservation Program.

Digital materials stored in these file formats should remain usable to researchers and administrative units at the University of Michigan for the foreseeable future and beyond. The Bentley Historical Library will therefore preserve the original version of content stored in these sustainable formats at the time of accession. Digital Curation Services will monitor community best practices and technological advances in case a migration to alternative preservation formats should prove necessary.

Visit http://fileinfo.com to find basic descriptions of file formats or search the PRONOM Technical Registry for format specifications and more in-depth information.

11/9/2011   1

Tier 2: Conversion of At-Risk Formats

The digital curation community has long acknowledged the disadvantages posed by proprietary formats (for which only specific software may be used) and content encoded with "lossy" compression (i.e. compression that reduces the quality of the data to conserve space). The Bentley Historical Library will therefore convert the most common at-risk formats to preservation-quality sustainable formats. To ensure the authenticity of materials, the original version will be maintained alongside the preservation copy.

See pp. 3-5 for a list of at-risk formats and preservation targets; these strategies reflect the policies and practices of peer institutions as well as the National Digital Information Infrastructure and Preservation Program. Visit the Library of Congress "Sustainability of Digital Formats" site (http://www.digitalpreservation.gov/formats/index.shtml) for more information on preservation issues and descriptions of preferred formats.

Tier 3: Bit-Level Preservation of All Other Formats

Because it is infeasible to create conversion plans for the tens of thousands of formats in existence, the Bentley Historical Library will ensure that digital holdings in other formats (i.e. ones not specifically identified in this document) will receive bit-level preservation. The use of integrity checks and regular replacement of storage media (conducted by trusted partners in the University of Michigan Library Information Technology division and Information and Technology Services) will preserve the raw data stored in these files (i.e. the "stream" of 0s and 1s) in its original state. The library concedes that hardware or software obsolescence may reduce the functionality of these files or render them inaccessible. At the same time, the faithful preservation of the content at the bit-level will allow the library to take advantage of future developments in emulation technology.

11/9/2011

2

Tier 1: Preservation of Sustainable Formats	Tier 2: Conversion Strategies for At-Risk Formats	Tier 3: Bit-Level Preservation
Raster Images		
• TIFF: Tagged Image Format File • JPEG/JFIF: Joint Photographic Experts Group JPEG Interchange Format File (lossy compression) • JPEG 2000: Joint Photographic Experts Group (lossless compression) • GIF: Graphic Interchange Format • PNG: Portable Network Graphic	Convert the following to TIFF: • BMP: Windows Bitmap • PSD: Adobe Photoshop Document • RAW: Raw Image Data File • FPX: FlashPix Bitmap • PCD: Kodak Photo CD Image • PCT: Apple Picture File • TGA: Targa Graphic	All others
Vector Images		
• SVG: Scalable Vector Graphics File	Convert the following to SVG: • AI: Adobe Illustrator • WMF: Windows Metafile PS: Convert the following to PDF: • PS: PostScript • EPS: Encapsulated PostScript	All others
Audio Files		
• MIDI: Musical Instrument Digital Interface File • XMF: Extensible Music File • WAV: Waveform Audio File Format • AIFF: Audio Interchange File Format • MP3: Moving Picture Experts Group Layer 3 compression • OGG: Ogg Vorbis Audio File • FLAC: Free Lossless Audio Codec File	Convert the following to WAV: • WMA: Windows Media Audio • RA/RM: Real Audio • SND: Apple Sound File • AU: Sun Audio File	All others

11/9/2011   3

<u>Tier 1</u>: Preservation of Sustainable Formats	<u>Tier 2</u>: Conversion Strategies for At-Risk Formats	<u>Tier 3</u>: Bit-Level Preservation
Video Files		
• <u>MPEG-1/2</u>: Moving Picture Experts Group • <u>AVI</u>: Audio Video Interleave File (uncompressed) • <u>MOV</u>: QuickTime Movie (uncompressed) • <u>MP4</u>: Moving Picture Experts Group (with H.264 encoding) • <u>MJ2</u>: Motion JPEG 2000 • <u>MXF</u>: Material Exchange Format File (uncompressed) • <u>DV</u>: Digital Video File (non-proprietary)	Convert the following to <u>MP4 (with H.264 encoding)</u>: • <u>SWF</u>: Shockwave Flash • <u>FLV</u>: Flash Video • <u>WMV</u>: Windows Media Video • <u>RV/RM</u>: Real Video	All others
Office Documents and Text Files		
• <u>DOCX</u>: MS Word Open XML Document • <u>XLSX</u>: MS Excel Open XML Document • <u>PPTX</u>: PowerPoint Open XML Document • <u>PDF</u>: Portable Document Format • <u>PDF/A</u>: Portable Document Format (Archival) • <u>TXT</u>: Plain Text File • <u>RTF</u>: Rich Text Format File • <u>XML</u>: Extensible Markup Language Data File • <u>CSV</u>: Comma Separated Values File • <u>TSV</u>: Tab Separated Values File	Convert the following to <u>Office Open XML</u>: • DOC: MS Word Document • XLS: MS Excel Document • PPT: PowerPoint Document	All others
Email		
• <u>MBOX</u>: Mailbox File	Convert the following to <u>MBOX</u>: • <u>EML</u>: Email Message • <u>PST</u>: Outlook Personal Information Store File • <u>Eudora</u> mail, etc. (40 total)	All others

11/9/2011   4

Tier 1: Preservation of Sustainable Formats	**Tier 2**: Conversion Strategies for At-Risk Formats	**Tier 3**: Bit-Level Preservation
Databases		
• SIARD: Software Independent Archiving of Relational Databases (open XML format) • CSV: Comma Separated Values File • MySQL SQL: Structured Query Language file; MySQL is an open source relational database management system	Convert the following into SIARD: • ACCDB or MDB: MS Access • SQL Server • Oracle Database	All Others

11/9/2011

5

OHIO STATE UNIVERSITY
Format Support
http://library.osu.edu/projects-initiatives/knowledge-bank/tools/format-support/

application/sgml	SGML	sgm, sgml	known
application/vnd.ms-excel	Microsoft Excel	xls	known
application/vnd.ms-powerpoint	Microsoft Powerpoint	ppt	known
application/vnd.ms-project	Microsoft Project	mpp, mpx, mpd	known
application/vnd.openxmlformats-officedocument.presentationml.presentation	Microsoft PowerPoint XML	pptx	known
application/vnd.openxmlformats-officedocument.spreadsheetml.sheet	Microsoft Excel XML	xlsx	known
application/vnd.openxmlformats-officedocument.wordprocessingml.document	Microsoft Word XML	docx	known
application/vnd.visio	Microsoft Visio	vsd	known
application/wordperfect5.1	WordPerfect	wpd	known
application/x-dvi	TeXdvi	dvi	known
application/x-filemaker	FMP3	fm	known
application/x-latex	LaTeX	latex	known
application/x-photoshop	Photoshop	psd, pdd	known
application/x-tex	Tex	tex	known
audio/x-aiff	AIFF	aif, aif, aifc	supported
audio/basic	audio/basic	au, snd	known
audio/x-mpeg	MPEG Audio	mpa, abs, mpeg, mp3	known
audio/x-pn-realaudio	RealAudio	ra, ram	known
audio/x-wav	WAV	wav	known
image/gif	GIF	gif	supported
image/jpeg	JPEG	jpeg, jpg	supported
image/png	PNG	png	supported
image/tiff	TIFF	tiff, tif	supported
image/x-ms-bmp	BMP	bmp	known
image/x-photo-cd	Photo CD	pcd	known
text/comma-separated	CSV	csv	supported
text/css	CSS File	css	known
text/html	HTML	html, htm	supported
text/plain	Text	txt, asc	supported
text/richtext	Rich Text Format	rtf	supported
text/xml	XML	xml	supported
video/mpeg	MPEG	mpeg, mpg, mpe	known
video/quicktime	Video Quicktime	mov, qt	known

Projects & Initiatives Knowledge Bank Center Tools Format Support

UNIVERSITY LIBRARIES

RUcore

Rutgers Community Repository

Archival standards for born-digital documents:
Recommended methods for keeping
stable preservation copies

Overview

As part of our plans to preserve student theses, dissertations, and newer editions of faculty texts and other culturally/academically significant documents, we inevitably will be tasked with preserving an increasing number of documents that originated electronically. These types of documents have been authored using various types of word processing and digital publishing software for decades, but the common practice had continued to be to print the final copy, and refer to the paper form as the final, finished product; the master original. Consequently, digital preservation would consist of scanning these analog objects back into a digital form, preserved electronically as scanned surrogates. Until very recently, we envisioned that scanning and digitizing from analog would comprise the bulk of how we digitally preserved all of our documents.

However, the increasing use of web-based publishing, online journals, and essentially paperless production has highlighted the benefits of seeking out the born-digital masters of preservation-worthy items whenever possible. Doing this affords us some advantages; namely, we can store the original in its most efficient digital form, often requiring less overhead and disk space while doing away with the quality challenges associated with scanning.

On the other hand, born digital preservation brings with it new challenges. Development of preservation standards for analog objects proved to be relatively simple, as the imaging industry laid much of the groundwork for us in terms of standardization across platforms. Further, development of future standards for digitized images, sound and video continues in an organized and orderly fashion, giving us plenty of time to contemplate migration to newer and better preservation formats.

Unfortunately, the same cannot be said for born digital documents. File formats for such objects vary widely, and the responsibility is upon us to identify a uniform set of file formats that we can adopt for preservation purposes.

As a result, a strategy for born digital document preservation must be adopted and followed that accomplishes the following:

- **Accurately renders** the formatting and content of the document, as intended by the creator of the document
- **Maintains stability** of the file format as well as possible. This may involve converting the document to archival formats, and storing both the original and the converted surrogate file.

Proposed Preservation Format Strategy: Multiple standards in play

Historically, born digital documents have been authored using a variety of different software packages, each with their own proprietary file formats. Early on, programs such as Wordstar, Wordperfect, Microsoft Works, ClarisWorks/AppleWorks, Adobe PageMaker, Quark Express, and others were distributed throughout the electronic document landscape.

More recently over the past decade, Microsoft Office has emerged as a de facto standard for general usage, with most businesses using it to create and distribute common document types. This usage has resulted in a trickle-down effect to the consumer level on home computers and in academia as well. MS Office isn't perfect, however. The file formats used by Microsoft have evolved over the years as new versions have been released, and inconsistencies exist between versions in how document formatting is rendered.

At present, there are a number of formats developed by various consortia that attempt to solve the problem of maintaining a persistent document standard, and Microsoft itself has sought to modernize and make their document formats a formally accepted industry standard. Some of the more prevalent solutions include:

- **OpenXML:** A standard developed and endorsed by Microsoft and a consortium of other commercial software vendors, and is the standard document format used in the Microsoft Office suite beginning with Office 2007. These documents are often recognizable by their .docx, xlsx, and .pptx extensions.

- **OASIS OpenDocument (ODF):** An existing, open standard for file formats in use primarily in open source and "non-Microsoft" environments. These file formats are the default for OpenOffice.org and similar Free Software alternatives.

- **Portable Document Format/Archival (PDF and PDF/A):** A well-established standard with roots in Adobe PDF, a subset of which is now an ISO standard and a Library of Congress recognized format for digital document preservation.

There is also significant prevalence of legacy standards, a majority of which consists of legacy MS Office document types (.doc, .xls, .ppt, etc.) as well as more complex file formats for more intricate or specialized document types (LaTeX, Adobe InDesign, Illustrator, etc.). And finally, there are a multitude of document authoring platforms that are currently supported but have smaller market shares, such as Apple's iWork, current versions of Corel WordPerfect

Our choice of standards are based the ability to endure as technological advances continue to develop, and a widespread acceptance is key to ensuring easy migrating to newer standards when the time comes to retire existing choices.

The Recommendation: Our best case to preserve born digital documents while retaining longevity

Considering the state of the born digital document landscape as outline above, it is thus advisable that more than one preservation datastream for born-digital objects is utilized when possible. This strategy permits us to build redundancy into our repository, and ensure that regardless of whether one standard "wins out" over the other, our objects will remain with at least one relevant archival datastream. With that in mind, our strategy can be outlined as follows:

1. **Store the original document in its native format** when possible.
   In most cases, this will be an MS Office document, or a file from a similarly well-known software package. In some instances, the document we receive may already be rendered as a PDF file, in which case Step 2 below may not be necessary.

2. **Store an additional surrogate master in the form of a PDF/Archival file.**
   Most modern document authoring software, including MS Office and OpenOffice.org, have a

built-in capability to accurately "export" a document into a PDF version. This capability should be used when available to generate a faithful PDF file. Otherwise, the PDF/A can be generated using software available on RUcore platform.

Why PDF/A: An established standard to augment object datastreams

Although Portable Document Format has its roots in a proprietary system, recent efforts have proven fruitful – mainly thanks to Adobe, the creator of the file format – to have it recognized as an archival standard. PDF/A is defined by ISO 19005-1:2005, an ISO Standard that was published on October 1, 2005. According to the Library of Congress: "PDF/A is suggested as a preferred format for page-oriented textual (or primarily textual) documents when layout and visual characteristics are more significant than logical structure."[1]

The openness of this format has permitted a widening selection of software solutions to create archival PDFs from most digital documents. As indicated earlier, PDF "export" capability now exists on the market leading packages. Additionally, some computing platforms, namely OS X for Apple Mac computers and Linux environments, have a similar "print to PDF" feature standard as part of the operating system. Finally, free viewers exist for desktop and mobile computing platforms. This heavy documentation and wide accessibility make PDF/A a natural choice for acting as platform-independent method for preserving and making accessible born digital documents, without requiring users to purchase expensive, proprietary software to view the content.

Review provisions for special cases

The diversity that exists among born digital document formats virtually guarantees that a single standard will not address all use cases. In particular, this standard will not be well-suited to born digital documents that are formatted in such a way that a page-based presentation approach would be detrimental. In such a case, a review of how these documents were constructed will have to be undertaken, and the Digital Data Curator will need to consult the Cyber Infrastructure Working Group (CISC) and related subgroups on the best way to proceed.

---

[1] http://www.digitalpreservation.gov/formats/fdd/fdd000125.shtml

IBB • RUCORE PRESERVATION STANDARDS • BORN DIGITAL DOCUMENTS   REV: 8/9/2010
PAGE 3 OF 3

RUcore

Rutgers Community Repository

Born Digital Still Images (Digital Photos):
Recommended Minimum Standards
For Archival and Presentation Datastreams

(Note: This document addresses standards for born-digital still images only. For standards and requirements pertaining to digitization, i.e. the scanning of paper, slides or other analog media into digital images, please refer to the RUcore Digital Surrogate Guidelines.)

Introduction and Rationale

Since the inception of RUcore, a significant shift in the field of photography has taken place, as amateurs and professionals alike have migrated *en masse* from analog film to digital formats. Since the first repository specifications for digital photography were drafted in 2006, we've seen digital photography overtake and dominate the field, largely overtaking film as a common medium for the capture of still images.

Of course, new objects will continue to be created using traditional film, and there is no foreseeable end to the creation of objects that originate on paper, film, or other analog recording format, even if those formats are relegated only to niche interest groups. To that end, the repository has established and refined a set of clear and concise standards that serve to acquire and preserve digital facsimiles of analog photographs, books and similar items.

Even so, digital photography brings with it new challenges and different capabilities than our existing core set of scanning digitization standards can support. As a result, an entirely separate set of standards dealing exclusively with digital photography and separate from those that support scanning must be defined and adhered to.

Emerging shifts to digital photography

While we have long heard that film's days are numbered, few have truly believed it until very recently. Digital photography has taken more than 12 years to mature, since the introduction of the first mass produced digital camera (the Apple Quicktake) in 1994. For a majority of this period, the switch from film to digital was largely relegated to early adopters, and broadly shunned by professionals who insisted film was here to stay. Within the last decade however, the quality of the hardware available as well as the introduction of professional grade software tools has not only swayed general opinion of digital photography, but has permitted digital photography to become a driving factor in the fate of most corporations in the field. Additionally, a number of very recent events has permanently and irrevocably spelled out that film's days as a dominant medium are numbered:

- **October 12, 2001**: Polaroid, Inc. files for bankruptcy. This is often seen as the watershed event for the decline of analog formats. Development of instant film formats stops, and while the popular Land Camera and a few other versions of Polaroid film survive, a wide array of other formats were discontinued.
  (Since 2001, Polaroid has been resurrected, filed for bankruptcy yet again, and the instant film formats discontinued. At present, private enthusiasts have attempted to revive Polaroid instant film through independent efforts.)

- **2001 – 2006**: Kodak has progressively discontinued a number of film formats, though it has stated it will aggressively pursue the continued manufacture of conventional 35mm and APS film. Additionally, Kodak announced in 2004 that while it "is, and will remain, committed to manufacturing and marketing the world's highest quality film," it is ending production of film cameras.

- **January 7, 2003**: Konica and Minolta, once both strong names in the film and film camera businesses respectively, announce they will merge to form a single company. This is largely viewed as the result of dwindling revenues from analog format sales, as both companies seek to share their digital technologies to strengthen their position in this market.

- **December 2005**: Kodak announces that for the first time, revenue from digital cameras and digital storage media has exceeded revenue from film-based sales.

- **January 11, 2006:** Nikon announces that is has discontinued all but two 35-mm Single Lens Reflex (SLR) cameras: The F6 and the FM10. It also announced it will discontinue the manufacture of all large format analog lenses, and all but nine interchangeable lenses to support the F6 and FM10. In addition, Nikon's photography division announces it will focus almost exclusively on the development of its digital product lines.

  As of 2010, the Nikon F6 and FM-10 continue to be manufactured, although the FM-10 is made by Cosina, and rebadged as a Nikon.

- **January 19, 2006:** Konica Minolta announces it will exit the photography business altogether, discontinuing both analog and digital film camera lines. It will sell its technology to Sony, which has indicated it will continue to support existing Konica Minolta digital camera lines, and develop new lenses compatible with the K-M lens mount.

- **July 22, 2009**: Kodak announces that it has manufactured its final batch of Kodachrome film after 74 years of production. Kodachrome was well known for its longevity and color stability. The last stocks of Kodachrome film have an expiration date of December, 2010.

- **January 2010**: Canon exits the analog film camera business by quietly discontinuing the manufacture of the EOS 1v. While remaining stocks of new EOS 1v cameras can still be purchased at retail stores, and while most lenses Canon makes for its digital cameras will still work on the film EOS line, all of the cameras Canon currently makes are digital-only.

- As of this year, digital images are estimated to account for 90 percent of all professionally taken photos according to market research firm InfoTrends.

At the same time that film-based companies are seeing the need to adapt or perish in the digital realm, digital cameras have improved dramatically in image quality. While there was once a time where the idea of using digital photographs to preserve images and keep permanent records was laughable, manufacturers are now producing affordable digital cameras – some aimed at entry-level users - that can meet or exceed the image quality produced by some 35mm film types.

These events point to one conclusion: analog film will continue to serve a greatly reduced role in the field of both amateur and professional photography as time progresses. While it is unrealistic to say that film will altogether become extinct, the prevalence of the common traditional formats (35mm, 110) are on the decline. It is very likely that film will be relegated to a limited range of formats for special-purposes applications and niche audiences, while more common general-use and utility-based photography will overwhelmingly shift to digital.

The need for baseline standards

The shift to digital photography has not been easy, and has been fraught with many painful lessons on what constitutes acceptable image quality. Indeed, early digital camera models produced images that were barely acceptable even for computer equipment of the time, much less for print media. Nonetheless, attempts were made by early adopters to use the technology for permanent preservation, and the results are that the digital images produced are unacceptable for viewing.

Indeed, for our purposes, digital cameras are only now being produced that can match the exacting standards that RUcore has laid out for acceptable, preservation-grade images. As the quality has improved, so has the acceptance and adoption of this hardware for general use photography. This is an important turning point for RUcore, as although our repository has a number of professional grade images in our collections, the majority of the photographs we have preserved thus far are often donated family photographs, amateur stills, and images that were generally produced using consumer equipment. As a result, we can expect that in the not-too-distant future, we may be expected to preserve amateur as well as professional digital images that are deemed to capture images and moments that are preservation-worthy.

In preparation for this, it is essential that RUcore adhere to a standard for which we will accept born digital images for inclusion in the repository.

Why have a separate standard from those for scanning photographs and documents?

At first glance, it might seem very easy to take the established standards for photograph and document digitization, and simply apply them as-is to digital photography. Indeed, the two processes share some similarities, and some of the requirements established for digitization should serve as the basis for establishing comparative standards for born digital still images. However, there are a few key differences between digital photography and analog digitization that make a broad application of a single standard impractical. Consequently, the two workflows need to be viewed from different paradigms to fully understand them and appreciate their differences.

Perspective is everything: digitization terms redefined

The best way to understand the differences between digital photography and digitization workflows is to view their intended purposes.

Digitization, or simply scanning, is intended to take an object recorded on an analog medium such as film, slides or paper. From this, we use an array of equipment and software to create a digital facsimile, with the intent of making the digital form represent the source object as accurately as possible. Consequently, the workflow, specifications and terminology are centered around this process.

Digital Photography on the other hand, is a process where the digital form *is* the primary, original storage medium. With digital photography, there is no physical medium that can accurately be described as the "original." In order for the digital format to take the primary role in recording and preservation, the hardware must be designed differently, and procedures and terminology have to take significantly different characteristics from digitization.

These differences in purpose and perspective result in important variations in how images are acquired and described:

Resolution: PPI vs. Megapixels: The most important difference between digitization and digital photography is the issue of resolution. Those familiar with digitization have grown accustomed to expressing resolution in terms of pixels per inch (ppi). This is because for digitization purposes, resolution is a function that expresses how accurately a scan will replicate the original. the higher the ppi, it is presumed, the higher the quality of the resulting digital image will be.

Digital photography, however, limits the relevance of ppi in terms of creating the original photograph. As image sensor sizes can vary greatly from one camera to the next, it is possible for two different camera models to arbitrarily assign widely different ppi values to their images, yet still produce digital images that are of comparable overall quality. In such a case, ppi only comes into play when a user wishes to print the digital image, in which case this value can be changed at will to suit the user's needs. As a result, the value of importance in digital photography is not how many pixels per inch make up an image, but the overall **pixel count**, or number of total pixels, that are used to represent the image. With current technology, this value is frequently expressed in Megapixels (MP).

Unaltered Originals: RUcore places the utmost importance on the ability to have an archival digital master, that is unaltered or unedited in any way. This requirement ensures that we can refer to this original at any time, should any edits or calibrations we perform on our derivate presentation versions of an object become unsuitable for display as technology changes. Producing such images are relatively easy when digitizing analog formats. The matter becomes trickier, however, when dealing with digital camera equipment.

Born Digital File Formats: JPG, RAW Image file formats and the unique challenges they present

To be sure, no single digital camera architecture will suit every photography application and so, camera vendors design and construct a vast assortment of digital cameras that vary in size, resolution and capability. A major challenge for dealing with digital photography is the diversity of equipment that is out in the field, and the resulting file formats that they generate.

Entry-Level Consumer Digital Cameras pose the greatest issue because they typically output files using the JPEG file format, with very lossy compression. To their credit, such cameras permit beginners and casual users to capture important and even historic moments with a minimum of effort and skill, and a great deal of archived content would not exist without casual photographers using such equipment, where more advanced and skilled photographers are simply not present. However, their ease also presents a disadvantage: entry-level cameras heavily process the images the capture, and the resulting image files are suboptimal for archival purposes without, at the very least, a file format change to an uncompressed TIFF format.

"Pro-sumer" and Professional Cameras typically provide the option to process and compress captured images into JPEG files similar to the consumer counterparts, but also tend to provide an option to yield *camera raw image files*. A camera raw image file contains minimally processed data as retrieved directly from the image sensor of the digital camera. Raw files are so named because they are not yet processed and therefore are not ready to be printed or edited with a bitmap graphics editor. Normally, the image is processed by conversion, where precise adjustments can be made before creating a "positive" file format such as an uncompressed TIFF or JPG file. Similar to a film negative, a raw digital image may have a wider dynamic range or contain more color information than can be provided using currently used file formats for presentation and access (TIFF, JPG, etc.), and preserves most of the information of the captured image. The purpose for a raw file is to achieve minimal loss of image data obtained from the sensor, and the conditions surrounding the capturing of the image (the technical metadata). In the field of photography, there is a pervasive, erroneous belief that RAW represents a single file format. In fact there are hundreds of raw image formats in use by different models of digital equipment, and the formats can vary from one vendor to the next, and even among different camera models made by the same manufacturer.

To get around the issue of non-standard and widely-disparate raw image formats, a standardized open file format, developed by Adobe Systems, Inc. and called "Digital Negative" (DNG) was developed in 2004, and is updated regularly with backward comaptibility. DNG is based upon the TIFF image standard, but encapsulates the additional sensor data in most proprietary raw image formats. In addition to Adobe software, the DNG file format is accessible and can be read by over 40 additional 3rd-party software packages across Windows, Mac and linux platforms. Because of this, RUcore tends to prefer capturing and preserving raw image files that have been converted to DNG, as these represented minimally-processed image files in an open, well-documented format that preserves not only an uncompressed digital image, but a wealth of associated technical metadata.

Recommended Born Digital Imaging Standards

Taking into account the aforementioned considerations, RUcore strives to adhere to the following recommendations for born digital still image content:

Resolution Requirements:

- **For entry-level consumer cameras:** *Minimum* of 7.0 <u>effective</u> Megapixels (MP), *or* **5.0 Megapixels if the camera has a "High Dynamic Range" (HDR) capability built-in.**
    - o Most entry-level "point and shoot" cameras heavily process and compress photos taken with them, introducing artifacts. Additionally, smaller imaging sensors in these cameras contribute to sensor noise. The high minimum resolution is necessary to help overcome these issues.
- **For "Pro-Sumer," bridge cameras, and professional dSLR cameras:** *Minimum* of 6.0 <u>effective</u> Megapixels (MP) *or* **5.0 Megapixels if the camera has a "High Dynamic Range" (HDR) capability built-in.**
    - o The resolution requirement for non-entry level cameras is lower because it is possible to obtain unprocessed, uncompressed images from these cameras, generally yielding better results even with less image information.
- **Additional considerations for both classes of cameras:**
    - o Use of "total" or "interpolated" pixel counts to meet the standard are *not* acceptable, when the effective count is below the minimum.

    - o A camera will *not* qualify as preservation-grade if it uses interpolation to reach its advertised resolution.
        - ▪ Example: A manufacturer advertises an extremely inexpensive digital camera capable of producing 10MP images, however the fine print indicates the camera is only equipped with a 3MP sensor. This camera is in fact interpolating a 3MP image to 10MP, and is not acceptable for preservation purposes.

- *Minimum* **8 bits per channel (24-bit color)**
    - o The camera should be capable of producing images using the sRGB palette.

- **The equipment *must* be capable of producing images with pixel dimensions of at least 3,000 pixels on one side.**
    - o Example dimensions: 3504 x 2336; 3072 x 2902; 3872 x 2592; and 3264 x 2448 are all acceptable.
- **The equipment must be EXIF compliant, version 2.0 or later.**
    - o EXIF compliance ensures the camera will embed metadata into the image file that details program modes, exposure settings, lens type, and other relevant information.

Image Format Requirements:

- **For consumer digital cameras: A direct copy of the JPG output file, without any post-processing.**
    - When possible, this JPG image will be directly converted to a TIFF file, without *any* changes to resolution, image quality, brightness/contrast, levels or other aspects.
    - An edited copy of a digital image is permitted if the edits are the direct result of the photographer's intent to present the image with such modifications for artistic effect. When permissible, an unedited "master" should also be preserved, but will not be made publicly accessible or viewable.

- **For ProSumer and professional cameras: The equipment should be able to produce images in RAW format.**
    - RAW image format ensures that the images produced by the camera are unprocessed, unedited and uncorrected.
    - The camera should either be able to produce image files conforming to the **Digital Negative (DNG)** file format, *or* interface with software that can export a DNG file from the camera's proprietary RAW format.
    Common software packages for this purpose: Adobe Photoshop, Adobe Lightroom. Additional listings of 3rd-party software packages can be found at http://www.adobe.com/products/dng/supporters.html
    - In addition to the DNG, a derivative TIFF file will be created and stored as a preservation format, through which presentation JPG, PDF and Djvu or Jpeg2000 images will be created for access by the public.
    - DNG permits the photographer to specify image and lighting adjustments, while not destructively altering the original image.

- **Alternately, the equipment should be able to produced uncompressed TIF images.**
    - Uncompressed TIFs can be used as an archival master, but bear in mind that DNG is the preferred format. Care should be taken when using TIFs to ensure that no image processing occurs to the TIF file, beyond what the camera performs internally. The same considerations will be made for artistic adjustments as in the treatment of camera-produced JPG files.

Other Considerations:

- **Image quality:** the equipment must be able to produce images with a minimum of sensor noise, and with optimal and accurate color reproduction. Such criteria is subjective, but generally most common photography equipment from major vendors will yield acceptable images as long as they meet the above specifications.
    When possible, a non-exclusive list of tested and known-good cameras will be maintained and made available.
- **Image stabilization:** If you choose a camera or lenses with Image Stabilization (IS), be certain the IS engine is of an "optical" variety, not "electronic" or "virtual." Optical IS uses floating internal lens optics and gyroscopes to ensure a steady image if the camera is moving. Electronic/Virtual IS uses software-based image editing and interpolation to artificially render a steady image.

o **Images taken from cameras not meeting the preservation spec:** It is inevitable that events will occur where images we wish to preserve in RUcore will be captured by cameras not meeting the above specifications. In the absence of better quality images, such images can be accepted by RUcore on a case-by-case basis, in which the RUL Digital Data Curator or the Digital Preservation Task Force will need to evaluate the images and determine the best course of action. It should be stressed however, that the viability of such images cannot be guaranteed and any preservation efforts will be done on a "best effort" basis.

RUcore
Rutgers Community Repository

Sound Objects:
Recommended minimum requirements
for preservation sampling of audio

Introduction

This document will set forth two standard requirements for audio. One will establish a minimum and recommended sampling rate – the quality level at which the audio is digitized – for the digital audio masters and presentation copies. The second standard will recommend specific file formats for the preservation master and derivatives, for implementation into the Workflow Management System (WMS).

Although the standards will be different, the philosophy behind preservation and presentation will be same as for all other object types. It will be mandatory to archive an uncompressed archival master, to ensure an object of the highest quality is preserved. Additionally, a small but diverse number of presentation copies will be archived as well. These presentation copies are to be stored and accessible in formats that the end user will find easy to play back, and will be "low-bandwidth friendly" whenever possible, allowing users with slower internet connections to have access to these objects as well.

Sampling and Digitization Rationale

As with all other objects, obtaining a high quality sample of the original for preservation in RU-CORE will assure the best chance of long term preservation without having to go back to the original source for a resample in the future. This will also allow us to ensure that the presentation copies provide a comparatively high fidelity that sacrifices little in quality. In the digital realm, audio is represented by a digital sampling at a set frequency, to obtain a granular but reasonably accurate representation of the analog original. Sampling is the process of converting a signal (e.g., a function of continuous time or space) into a numeric sequence (a function of discrete time or space). The higher the sampling rate – it is assumed – the more accurate the digital representation will be.

For audio, there has been a wide practice of following the *Nyquist-Shannon Sampling Theorem*, a doctrine which is used to assert that 44.1kHz is an acceptable minimum sampling rate for all audio. This belief is based on the established fact that most human ears perceive sound up to an upper frequency threshold of 20,000Hz, and sampling must occur at twice the upper limit to achieve an acceptable digital copy. Consequently, a number of digital recordings, including CDs, adhere to this standard sampling rate (thus the term "CD Quality" is attributed to this sampling rate).

This 44.1kHz sampling rate is not without its detractors. Over time, audiophiles have consistently complained that they perceive a loss of fidelity when analog recordings are digital remastered to CD Audio. While some audio experts have insisted that these complaints are based on purely psychological factors, there is some support for a need for a higher sampling rate. There are inherent risks in losing quality to the sampling process, causing a degradation that is not accounted for in Nyquist. However, a higher sampling rate may be able to compensate for these sampling losses.

As a result, the standard set forth accounts for the CD-Audio minimum sampling rate and accepts it as a minimum, while recommending a higher level whenever the opportunity to sample at a better rate presents itself.

Recommended Standards for NJDH and RU-CORE Audio Sampling

- **Minimum sampling rate: 44.1kHz 16-bit (CD Audio)**
  This is the minimum acceptable rate to ensure a good preservation master. Most Compact Discs (CDs) are mastered at this rate. As such, all audio obtained from CDs will be archived at this rate. Additionally, 44.1kHz is a suitable sampling rate for RU-Core partners when mastering recordings of spoken-word speech (i.e. interviews, speeches, press conferences and lectures), that are not accompanied by high-fidelity sound or music.

- **Recommended Sampling rate: 96kHz, 24-bit audio**
  This is widely considered an ideal rate for high quality audio recordings, including DVD-Audio. For most audio formats, this sampling rate is the maximum sampling rate that also supports Quad (Dolby 4.0) and Surround (5.1) audio. When repository content partners are making a first generation sample of musical or high-fidelity recordings from an analog master, it is recommended that this sampling rate be used whenever technically possible.

- **High Level (Maximum) Sampling rate: 192kHz, 24-bit audio**
  This sampling rate is often touted by audiophiles as one of the best sampling rates to work with in the editing of audio recordings and creating master samples. However, this format is generally not supported in current mass-produced formats for Quad or Surround sound. As such, recordings sampled at this rate should be limited to Mono or Stereo recordings. In general, this sampling rate, and higher rates, are recommended if there is a reasonable justification for using such a high sampling rate, and it is believed that the 96kHz rate will not be sufficient for accurate reproduction of the original sound.

Recommended File formats for preservation and presentation of audio objects

The following formats are recommended for the preservation and presentation of audio.

- **For Preservation: Standard WAV or Broadcast WAV Format (BWF)**
  BWF is an extension of the popular WAV audio format. It was first specified by the European Broadcasting Union in 1997, and updated in 2001. WAV records audio using Pulse Code Modulation (PCM), the industy standard method for digitizing audio and is used in CDs and DVDs.
  The stated purpose of these two file formats is the seamless exchange of digitized audio between different computer platforms. BWF also specifies additional metadata, allowing audio processing elements to identify themselves, document their activities, and permit synchronization with other recordings. This metadata is stored as an extension chunk in an otherwise standard digital audio WAV file.

- **No compression of archival master is recommended**
  As of this writing, the Audio and Video Standards Working Group recommends that no compression of the preservation master occur. While there are some lossless compression formats available (e.g. Shorten and FLAC), the open source formats that are currently available are not mature, nor do they have a large enough user base to justify their use. Doing so may expose the repository to the risk of being unable to later decompress and access these masters if at some point in the future, support and development for the chosen compression scheme is abandoned. However, the working group does recommend that the issue of lossless compression for archival masters be re-assessed at a later date, to determine whether an open standard is more widely accepted, likely to be readily available and supported for the foreseeable future, and suits our needs.

AUDIO/VIDEO STANDARDS WORKING GROUP:
I. BEARD, I. BOGUS, N. GONZAGA, B. NAHORY, R. SANDLER   2   RU-CORE AND NJDH STANDARDS ANALYSIS FOR AUDIO OBJECTS
LAST UPDATE: 8/9/2010

148 · Representative Documents: Format Policies

- **For presentation Audio: MP3 or Ogg Vorbis, using Variable Bitrate (VBR) encoding**
  Both file formats are widely used by computer end users and supported by most popular audio playback hardware and software.

  MP3 enjoys wider acceptance, but is a format that is encumbered by proprietary compression algorithms. However, current licensing restrictions indicate that we would not be required to pay royalties for non-commerical, non-profit-generating use. Ogg Vorbis, while not quite as widely accepted, still enjoys support from the audiophile community and is an open source format, without any proprietary encumberances. The drawback however, is that Ogg Vorbis is not natively supported by common players such as Windows Media Player, Apple Quicktime, and some mobile devices.

  For this reason, MP3 is the current standard presentation audio format for RUcore.

Evaluating collection objects that do not meet standards

The working group recognizes that there has been a period of at least two decades where digital audio has been recorded and exists prior to the establishment of these guidelines. It is important to acknowledge that there is a prevalence of digital audio objects that may be of immense value to repository partners, but for which there is no analog master available and the best digital master may not meet our established digitization standards.

In light of this, it is important to stress that the standards we have established are recommendations, and must not be the only criteria for accepting or dismissing a potential audio object. While we believe it is of the utmost importance that collection partners strive to meet the standards in order to ensure longevity of their collections, the advisory committee should consider the overall content and value of the collection before making a decision as to its inclusion. In particular, the committee may want to evaluate:

- The playback quality of the objects, and whether the audio quality can subjectively be deemed acceptable in spite of not meeting standards.
- The importance, prominence, and significance of the content
- Whether further degradation of the content can be inhibited by storing the object as an archival master, or converting an object with lossy compression into a lossless format.

If the advisory committee decides that the benefits of storing an object or collection into the repository outweigh its lack of standards compliance, then the standards can be waived for that object or collection. However, in doing so, the point should be stressed to the collection partner that long term preservation of the object *cannot* be guaranteed. While the repository and the team supporting it will put forth its best efforts to sustain the collection, the collection partner should be made aware that the chances of losing the object to format obsolescence or degradation of integrity are greatly increased because the object has not been digitized to our specifications.

Video and Moving Image Objects:
Recommended Minimum Standards
For Archival and Presentation Datastreams

Introduction

This document will set forth a standards recommendation for moving images and digital video. In particular, this video object standard will recommend specific file formats for the preservation master and derivatives, for implementation into the Rutgers Community Repository (RUcore) and projects using similar architectures, as well as recommend sampling rates and specifications for presentation derivatives.

As with all other standard types established thus far, it will be mandatory to store and preserve an archival master, to ensure an object of the highest available quality is maintained for digital preservation. Additionally, one or more downsampled and compressed presentations copies will be made available for end users wishing to access these objects online. These presentation copies are to be stored and accessible in formats that users will find easy to play back, and will use file formats and codecs that are compatible with multiple computer platforms, using established industry standards.

Sampling and Digitization Rationale

The handling and preservation of digitized moving images presents a unique challenge to digital repositories. Presently, uncompressed digital video demands an extremely large amount of storage space, and produces incredibly large files. Yet, the need to store an uncompressed or reliable lossless-compressed object is paramount to ensure its longevity. While it is recognized that work continues in perfecting lossless video compression standards, we feel that these codecs are not mature enough and have not yet reached a critical mass in terms of user base and supporting software to implement in place of an uncompressed stream. We remain open to revisiting this stance in the future.

We also recognize with the growing convergence of digital devices, and the prevalence of smaller video capture equipment, there will be an increasing amount of digital content which is born in a compressed digital format. Such cases will pose long-term preservation challenges depending on the file times, video codecs, resolution and compression levels used. When such video is slated for inclusion into RUcore, a case-by-case condition analysis will occur; best efforts will be made to store the native format as an archival datastream; and when necessary, a converted copy into a designated stable format will also be stored with the archival datastream.

In spite of the present need to store an uncompressed stream when digitizing from an analog master, it is obvious that delivering such an object to end users would be impractical given current average connection speeds. Consequently, there is an additional need for downsampled, compressed presentation formats for video objects, more than any other object type addressed by the repository.

As always, the guidelines presented here are recommendations, and there may be cases where judgment calls will need to be made about objects that would be better preserved by modifying the recommended guidelines for this purpose. In particular, the digitization team has not yet digitized film archives, and as such those formats will need to be analyzed for the best possible digitization settings. The Digital Data Curator, as well as the Digital Preservation Task Force, should be consulted for guidance when such adaptations are required.

RUCORE MEDIA STANDARDS WORKING GROUP:
I. BEARD, I. BOGUS, E. GORDER, N. GONZAGA, B. NAHORY, R. SANDLER

RUCORE AND NJDH STANDARDS ANALYSIS FOR MOVING IMAGE OBJECTS
VERSION 4 – LAST REVIEWED 9 AUGUST 2010

Recommended Standards for NJDH and RUcore Video Digitization

For analog preservation masters (when possible):
File format: *Uncompressed, Full Frame Video (AVI file format) or DV Source for digital video.*

Frame rate for analog Standard Definition (SD) video, NTSC: *29.97 frames per second, 640 x 480 resolution (assuming square pixels). 4:2:2 quantization, 25MiB/s data rate.*
We recognize this sampling scheme as the best practical standard to ensure a good preservation master of analog SD video archives, and will be the most common digitization sampling rate for objects that come to us as SD analog video. This standard is based on our experiences with digitizing videotaped objects.

For Digital objects (i.e. DV/HDV), including high definition video: *Use and preserve same frame rate, resolution and bit rate as the original.*
For born-digital video objects such as DV or MPEG-2, the logical course of action is to preserve the exact specifications of the original. It will not be wise to downsample the original as that will cause a loss of object data, and no improvement in quality will be gained from upsampling.

All other objects: Make best effort to preserve frame rate and resolution of the original content. The goal in digitizing the various analog formats that may come to us will be to create a digital master file that preserves the content of the analog original as accurately as the digital media permits. A wide degree of flexibility and some experimentation may be required to determine accurate settings for each unique case.

Presentation video files:

- **One streaming/progressive downloadable video clip:**
  - **MPEG-4 H.264 video (.MOV, .M4V, .MP4), encoded for hinted streaming**
  - For 4:3 – Minimum of **640 x 480 resolution (square pixels), 30 frames per second, multi-pass encoding**
  - For 16:9 - Minimum of **854 x 480 resolution (square pixels), 30 frames per second, multi-pass encoding**
  - Recommended Data rate of **640 kbps minimum, and up to 860 kbps.**
    Use higher bitrates for videos with more detail and greater motion.
  - **Key frames inserted every 30 frames at minimum, or auto-select. This rate should be adjusted when necessary for best results.**

  This recommendation is aimed at balancing the file size, and the amount of bandwidth required to play the video, while trying not to sacrifice video quality. This specification necessitates the use of a broadband internet connection, but is configured so that basic Home DSL or casual WiFi users should still be able to view the content.

  MPEG-4 Video, particularly MP4, is cross-platform and can be accessed by desktop computer users of varying operating systems (Windows, Mac, Linux), using free software and established web standards. H.264 video is also viewable on a multitude of internet-connected mobile devices.

  Starting in late 2010, the MP4 container format is recommended, as this format permits us to use a single H.264 video file to provide service for mobile devices as well as progressive download and streamed video.

RUCORE MEDIA STANDARDS WORKING GROUP: RUCORE AND NJDH STANDARDS ANALYSIS FOR MOVING IMAGE OBJECTS
I. BEARD. I. BOGUS. E. GORDER. N. GONZAGA. B. NAHORY. R. SANDLER   VERSION 4 – LAST REVIEWED 9 AUGUST 2010

Progressive download standard for older objects

Prior to September 2010, the standard for progressive-download presentations videos were as follows, but has since been deprecated with the use of the single-source MP4 spec listed above:

- **If permissions permit: one progressive-download video clip**
    - **Flash Video Format (.FLV), using ON2VP6 Codec**
    - For 4:3 – Minimum of **640 x 480 resolution (square pixels), 30 frames per second, multi-pass encoding**
    - For 16:9 - Minimum of **854 x 480 resolution (square pixels), 30 frames per second, multi-pass encoding**
    - Data rate of **512 kbps**
    - **Key frames inserted every 30 frames. This rate should be adjusted when necessary.**

Our experimentation has shown these output settings to be an ideal compromise, producing a clip viewable at acceptable quality on a computer screen while providing a reasonably manageable file size. Users choosing to view this format will need to download the latest version of a free Macromedia Flash Plug-in, provided by Adobe Systems, Inc.

Workflows

Accessioning Workflow
1. Donor Agreement received
2. Media physically secured (create separation sheets if necessary to preserve original order)
3. Record accession information AT
4. Assign Barcode (use double barcodes for separation sheets as appropriate)
5. Photograph media
6. Acquire media content (disk image or copy)
7. Record checksums
8. Scan content for PII & Viruses
    Exceptions
        i. Check donor agreements for existing policies
        ii. If none apply: negotiate restriction, return, or destruction with donor
        iii. Comply with agreements
        iv. Record restrictions & actions taken
9. Move content to Dark Storage
10. Securely erase local copy

General Policies
- Electronic media received by RBMSCL should only be accessed in read-only mode
    Media with a USB interface must use the write-blocker
    Firewire & eSATA drives must be mounted in read-only mode
- No media received by RBMSCL shall be reused for any other purpose.
- Electronic media shall never leave the custody of RBMSCL/UA except for:
    Preservation activities (e.g. specialized data recovery services) under the direction of the Electronic Records Archivist (requires the use of a signed transfer form)
    Very large volume transfers copying to ITS secure network storage by ITS staff under the direction of the Electronic Records Archivist (requires the use of a signed transfer form)
- All media should be clearly marked with the accession number and/or collection name.
    Label bands or dedicated storage boxes with labels are preferred. Avoid directly labeling the media if possible.
- If there is an unavoidable delay in transferring the data to the secure network storage, a record for the data will be added to the electronic media transfer queue so that the need for the transfer is documented and attended to in a timely manner.
- RBMSCL/UA transfer drives (used by archivists visiting the donor):
    Shall be clearly labeled
    Used only by permission of the Electronic Records Archivist
    Shall be cleared only after transfer to ITS secure network storage has been verified and then only by the Electronic Records Archivist
    Archivists shall request the donor NOT purge copied files until transfer has been verified

Seth Shaw — last modified Jul 20, 2011 04:13 PM

Bentley Historical Library Digital Processing Manual

Table of Contents

Introduction

This processing manual provides guidance and instructions for the processing of digital materials at the Bentley Historical Library (BHL). Procedures, tools, and the overall digital processing workflow are subject to change due to advances in professional best practices, the development of resources in the digital curation community, and the Bentley Library's ongoing collaboration with the University of Michigan Library Information Technology division. In addition to revisions that take place as BHL Digital Curation Services implements digital processing procedures, this manual will be reviewed on an annual basis.

The BHL *Digital Processing Manual* details procedures that will take place from the initial transfer and appraisal of content to archival custody through the eventual deposit of material in a long-term digital repository. Digital Curation Services advocates a *More Product, Less Process* approach to handling digital records and emphatically notes that processing archivists and student processors will not be able to deal with content on an individual file level. The BHL digital processing workflow instead relies upon a number of micro-services that will perform batch operations on digital accessions. In addition to traditional archival procedures such as the appraisal, arrangement, separation, and description of content, digital processing for long-term preservation requires the following:

- Migration of content from removable media
- Capture
- Virus scans
- Renaming
- File format conversion
- Personally-identifiable information scans
- Creation of ZIP archives
- File characterization
- Message digest calculation

The various steps in the digital processing workflow produce log files that will be preserved as metadata for the digital accession. It is of the utmost importance that the steps and procedures outlined in this manual—from file naming conventions for log files to settings used in application—be strictly followed by all BHL employees engaged in the processing of digital content. In addition, processing archivists and student processors will produce descriptive, administrative, and preservation metadata that will permit the Bentley Library to generate a Metadata Encoding and Transmission Standard (METS) document for each digital deposit.

Progress on each digital deposit will be tracked with the Bentley Historical Library Digital Processing Checklist, a document that will reside in the *Metadata*\\ folder.

Workflow: Overview

The basic workflow for processing digital records will involve the following steps:

1. UARP/MHC reaches an agreement with a donor/creator regarding the transfer of digital content to the Bentley Historical Library.

2. Archivists are provided access to digital materials (either remotely or via removable storage media).

3. A preliminary review of the digital materials will be performed (if it has not taken place prior to the transfer agreement) to determine if they warrant additional processing and long-term preservation by the Bentley Historical Library. Archivists will also confirm the presence of sensitive materials that will require restrictions under applicable laws and/or BHL policies.

4. Create an accession record in BEAL. If some/all of the digital content will not be processed for long-term preservation, note these materials in the separations.

5. Digital Curation Services will manage the creation of and access to appropriate processing directories in the Interim Repository.

6. Content will be migrated to the appropriate processing directory in the Interim Repository.
   a. Depending on the source/transfer method, archivists will use one of several tools identified and tested by Digital Curation Services.
   b. Processing directory will include a \Metadata\ folder.
   c. Create a separations folder (titled: CollectionID_Name) in \bhl-root\Separations\
   d. Note the unprocessed location in BEAL and record the capture of content in the PREMIS preservation event spreadsheet.

7. Following a *More Product, Less Process* approach, the archivist/student processor will conduct the following operations:
   a. Change filename to the Deposit ID (the collection ID plus a four digit number, i.e. 87134_0001)
   b. Virus scan (Save log file in the \Metadata\ folder and record event in the PREMIS preservation event spreadsheet.)
   c. Backup of content
   d. Normalization of folder/file names (Save log file in the \Metadata\ folder and record event in the PREMIS preservation event spreadsheet.)
   e. Scan for personally identifiable information (PII) (Save log file in the \Metadata\ folder and record event in the PREMIS preservation event spreadsheet.)

  f. Appraisal and analysis of content (If email is present, archivist may need to convert file format to MBOX to review messages in an MBOX viewer.)

  g. Add file extensions to unidentified files with TRiD (Save log file in the \Metadata\ folder and record event in the PREMIS preservation event spreadsheet.)

  h. Separation of unnecessary or superfluous content
    i. Use TreeSize to identify and move content to appropriate folder in \bhl-root\Separations\
    ii. Save log file in the Metadata folder and record event in the PREMIS preservation event spreadsheet.

  i. Arrangement (only if needed)

  j. Run bhl_batch.bat to create preservation copies of material in at-risk formats.
    i. Text/office documents: MS Word, Excel, and PowerPoint documents will be migrated to 2010 Office Open XML; PDF documents will be converted to PDF/A.
    ii. Raster Images: BMP, PSD, PCD, PCT, and TGA will be converted to TIFF.
    iii. Raw Camera Images: 3FR, ARW, CR2, DCR, MRW, NEF, ORF, PEF, RAF, RAW, and X3F will be converted to JPEG (for access)
    iv. Vector Images: AI, EMF, and WMF will be converted to SVG; PS and EPS will be converted to PDF/A.
    v. Audio files: WMA, RA, SND, and AU will be converted to WAV.
    vi. Video files: FLV, WMV, RMVB, and RV will be converted to MPEG4 (with H.264 encoding).
    vii. Email will be converted to MBOX.
    viii. Database files: ACCDB, MDB, SQL Server and Oracle DB will be converted to SIARD open XML.

  k. Create ZIP archive files (if necessary) and finalize packaging of content for deposit in a long-term preservation repository

  l. Content characterization with DROID

8. Content will be transferred to a post-processing location
  a. Restricted content: \bhl-archive\ ("dark" storage location)
  b. Unrestricted content: \bhl-root\deepblue_deposits\ in the Interim Repository

9. Complete metadata forms
  a. Deep Blue deposit spreadsheet
  b. PREMIS preservation event spreadsheet
  c. EAD descriptive and administrative metadata template

10. If the content is unrestricted, Digital Curation Services will coordinate its deposit in Deep Blue.

11. For unrestricted material, place a copy of the deposit (with *Metadata*\\ folder) in *bhl-archive*\\.

12. Description:
    a. Create/update finding aid
    b. Create/update catalog record
    c. Update BEAL record

13. Clean up:
    a. Manage disposition of separations, per the transfer agreement.
    b. Delete backup copy
    c. Delete version from 'Unprocessed' and *deepblue_deposits*\\ directories (if applicable).

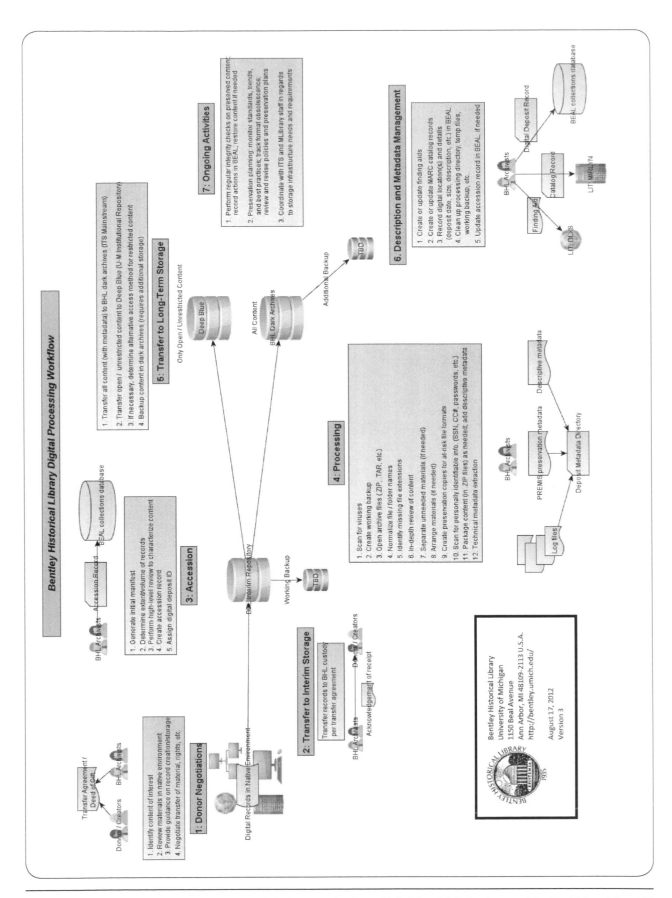

Bentley Historical Library Web Archives:
Methodology for the Acquisition of Content

Nancy Deromedi and Michael Shallcross
Digital Curation

Version 2.0 (August 2, 2011)

Table of Contents

1

Introduction

The Bentley Historical Library's Digital Curation Division has developed a
methodology and workflow for the acquisition of content. These procedures are
based on the available features of the California Digital Library (CDL)'s Web
Archiving Service (WAS) as well as standard archival practices (such as appraisal
and description). This document provides an overview of the Bentley Historical
Library's methodology for website preservation.

The actual process of website preservation may be broken down into three main
steps:

1. Identification of the crawl target
2. Configuration of the crawler settings
3. Contextualization of content

Guided by collecting priorities, surveys of relevant websites, and knowledge of
significant individuals and organizations, archivists identify potential targets for
preservation. By standardizing the configuration of web crawler settings and
addition of metadata and descriptions, archivists are able to ensure that websites
are preserved in a manner that is consistent, efficient, and cost-effective.

Given the fast pace of change in web archiving technology and ongoing development
of features and functionalities in WAS, this methodology document will be reviewed
on an annual basis and revised accordingly.

August 2, 2011   2

Identification of Content

The Bentley Historical Library employs the Heritrix web crawler (also known as a spider or robot) to copy and preserve websites. As a subscriber to WAS, the Bentley Library relies upon an implementation of Heritrix specially configured and maintained by the CDL. A web crawler is an application that starts at a specified URL and then methodically follows hyperlinks to copy html pages and associated files (images, audio files, style sheets, etc.) as well as the websites underlying structure. The initiation of a web capture requires the archivist to specify one or more seed URLs from which the web crawling application will preserve the target site.

Accurate and thorough website preservation requires the archivist to become familiar with a site's content and architecture in order to define the exact nature of the target. This attention to detail is important because content may be hosted from multiple domains. For example, the University of Michigan's Horace H. Rackham School of Graduate Studies hosts the majority of its content at http://www.rackham.umich.edu/ but maintains information on academic programs at https://secure.rackham.umich.edu/academic_information/programs/. To completely capture the Rackham School's online presence, archivists needed to identify both domains as seed URLs.

At the same time, multiple domains present on a site may merit preservation as separate websites. For example, the University of Michigan's Office of the Vice President of Research (http://research.umich.edu/) maintains a large body of information related to research administration (http://www.drda.umich.edu/) and human research compliance (http://www.ohrcr.umich.edu/). Although these latter sites could be included as secondary seeds for the Vice President of Research's site, their scope and informational value led archivists to preserve them separately.

Once the target of the crawl has been identified and defined, the archivist enters the seed URL(s) and site name in the WAS curatorial interface (see Figure 1).

Figure 1

The Bentley Historical Library standardizes the names of preserved sites by using the title found at the top of the target web page or, in the absence of a formal/adequate title, the name of the creator (i.e. the individual or organization responsible for the intellectual content of the site). The library follows the best practices for collection titles as established by Describing Archives: a Content

August 2, 2011   3

Standard (DACS); to ensure that the nature of the collections are clear, archivists supply "Web Archives" in the final title. The University Archives and Records Program (UARP) furthermore includes "University of Michigan" in titles to highlight the provenance of websites. Complete names for sites in the University of Michigan Web Archives thus follow the pattern "Board of Regents Web Archives (University of Michigan)."

August 2, 2011

4

Configuration of Web Crawler Settings

WAS utilizes the open-source web crawler Heritrix to archive websites. As a command-line tool, this application allows for a wide range of user settings; the curatorial interface in WAS provides for a more-limited number of options. For each crawl, archivists may adjust the following settings:

- **Scope:** defines how much of the site will be captured. The archivist may elect to capture the entire host site (i.e. http://bentley.umich.edu/), a specific directory (i.e. http://bentley.umich.edu/exhibits/), or a single page (i.e. a letter written by Abbie Hoffman to John Sinclair, featured at http://bentley.umich.edu/exhibits/sinclair/ahletter.php) (see Figure 2).

Figure 2

To thoroughly capture target websites, the Bentley Historical Library generally uses the "Host site" setting, unless the target is a single directory located on a more extensive host or a specific page.

Linked pages: determines whether or not content from other hosts/URLs will be captured; archivists have two options for this setting. If set to "No," the crawler will only archive materials on the seed URL entered by the archivist; if "Yes," the crawler will follow hypertext links one 'hop' to capture linked resources. Capturing linked pages will not result in an indefinite crawl (in which the robot follows link after link after link); instead, the crawler will only capture the page (and embedded content) that is specified by the hypertext link. No additional content on this latter site will be crawled.

To avoid preserving extraneous content, the Bentley Historical Library by default does not captures linked pages. Archivists will only capture linked pages if it required as a result of website design or if it is necessary to capture contextual information for a high priority web crawl.

Maximum time: specifies the maximum duration of a crawl. The archivist may select "Brief Capture (1 hour)" or "Full Capture (36 hours)" and the crawl will continue until all content has been preserved (in which case it may end early) or the allotted time period has elapsed. If a session times out before the crawler has finished, the resulting capture may be incomplete.

To avoid missing content due to time restrictions, the Bentley Historical Library uses the "Full Capture" option by default. Archivists use the "Brief Capture" if the target involves a limited amount of content and the additional crawl time would result in unnecessary content (for instance, the archivist only wants to capture a blog's most recent posts and is not interested in the entire site).

- **Capture frequency**: designates how often a crawl will be repeated. The archivist may elect to crawl a site once or configure the robot to perform daily, weekly, monthly, or custom captures (see Figure 3).

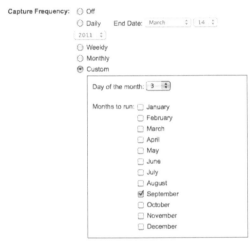

Figure 3

Archivists generally choose the "Custom" option and select an annual capture date, being mindful of important events/dates that might result in updates to the target site. (For instance, University of Michigan sites are captured near the beginning or end of the academic year.) This strategy is particularly effective with 'aggregative' websites in which new content is placed at the top/front of pages while older information is moved further down the page or placed in an 'archive' section. For high priority targets (such as the University of Michigan Office of the President) or sites with a large turnover of important content, captures may be scheduled on a more frequent basis.

As the foregoing discussion reveals, the accurate and effective configuration of crawl settings must be based on the archivist's appraisal of content and understanding of the target site's structure. The failure to consider these factors may lead to a capture that, on the one hand, is narrowly circumscribed and incomplete or, on the other, is unnecessarily broad and filled with superfluous information.

August 2, 2011   6

Contextualization of Content

After the configuration of crawl settings, archivists supply each website with a description, metadata, and tags to help contextualize the preserved content and facilitate access.

Description:

WAS provides a 'Site Description' field so that archivists may contextualize preserved websites with an overview of the creator and/or subject matter (see Figure 4).

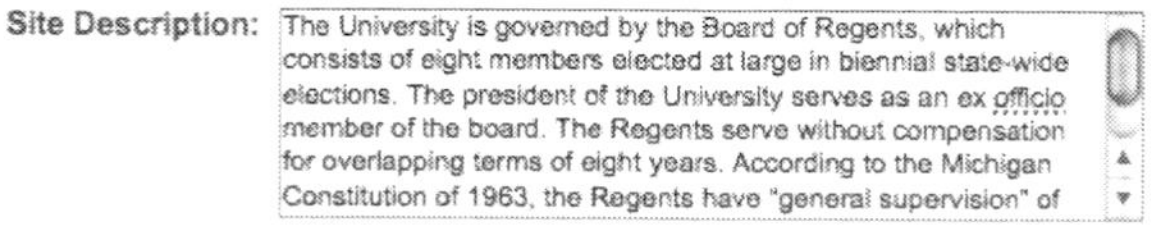

Site Description:
The University is governed by the Board of Regents, which consists of eight members elected at large in biennial state-wide elections. The president of the University serves as an ex officio member of the board. The Regents serve without compensation for overlapping terms of eight years. According to the Michigan Constitution of 1963, the Regents have "general supervision" of

Figure 4

To ensure accurate descriptions, archivists often use text supplied by the websites in an "About Us" or "More Information" section, if it is available. Patrons have ready access to this information from each page in the web archives under the "Show Details" tab (see Figure 5).

University of Michigan Web Archives
Title: Regents of the University of Michigan
Archival URL: http://webarchives.cdlib.org/sw1xd0rf0p/http://regents.umich.edu/
Date captured: 08/16/10 02:38 PM
About this archive
Dates: 08/16/10 02:38 PM
show document
show details
help
This document is an archived copy for study and research. The original may be available at http://regents.umich.edu/
UNIVERSITY OF MICHIGAN

Figure 5

August 2, 2011 7

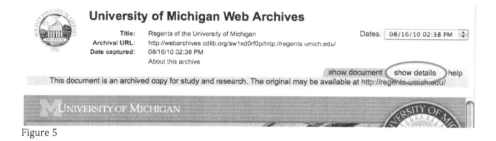

Metadata

The WAS curatorial interface permits archivists to enter information related to the "Creator," "Publisher," "Subjects," and "Geographic coverage" of each site (see Figure 6).

Creator: Board of Regents

Publisher: The Regents of the University of Michigan

Subjects: University of Michigan--Administration

Geographic coverage: Michigan--Ann Arbor

Figure 6

Although WAS intended these metadata fields to mirror elements in the Dublin Core Metadata Set, the Bentley Historical Library needed to establish local definitions and conventions. After extensive discussions among archivists, the following practices were adopted:

- *Creator* denotes the individual or organization that generated or supplied the website's intellectual content (and not merely the web designer who created the page).

- *Publisher* refers to the entity ultimately responsible for the production and presentation of content. Although the publisher may often be identical to the creator, the Regents of the University of Michigan are recognized as the collective publisher for all sites affiliated with the university. Similar situations may arise with other archived websites.

- *Subjects* express Library of Congress subject authorities that correspond to MARC21 6XX fields. Due to the lack of formatting in this field (and the indeterminate status of their use within WAS), the Bentley Historical Library does not include indicators and subfield codes but instead simply enters the primary and secondary descriptors and separates them with double hyphens.

- *Geographic coverage* identifies where the activities described in the site took place. Archivists again utilized MARC21 conventions so that the main geographic entry is followed by the subdivision but did not (for reasons stated above) include the field codes themselves.

August 2, 2011   8

Tags

WAS also allows archivists to "tag" archived websites with one or more subject terms to facilitate user access to content. Archivists have therefore created tags that identified significant groups of interrelated content: for example, the "College of Engineering" tag identifies all archived websites that are created, maintained, or associated with this particular college. When browsing the site list of a public archives, a user may select a tag to review only those archived websites associated with a specific subject (see Figure 7).

Figure 7

Tags are currently employed in both the Bentley Historical Library Web Archives; additional ones will be created as the collections continue to expand and as archivists receive feedback from users. Management features in the curatorial interface allow archivists to modify or delete tags; all sites that are denoted by the affected tags will inherit these changes (see Figure 8).

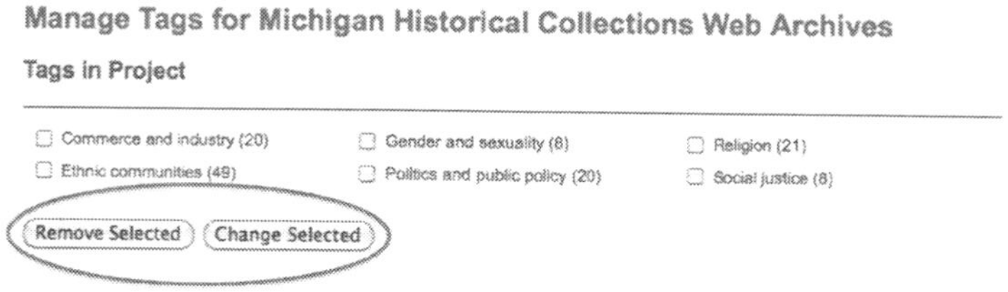

Manage Tags for Michigan Historical Collections Web Archives

Tags in Project

☐ Commerce and industry (20)	☐ Gender and sexuality (8)	☐ Religion (21)
☐ Ethnic communities (49)	☐ Politics and public policy (20)	☐ Social justice (8)

(Remove Selected) (Change Selected)

Figure 8

Many sites in the web archives do not have tags because they do not fit into these established categories and tagging is only effective when there are a significant number (i.e. five or more) of related sites. Archivists may, however, add tags to existing archived websites should the need arise.

With the inclusion of description, metadata, and tags, the archivist may initiate the web crawl and successfully conclude the workflow for content acquisition. Archivists regularly meet to discuss the status of the web archives and review difficult appraisal and content management decisions.

August 2, 2011   9

Quality Assurance for Bentley Historical Library Web Archives: Guidelines and Procedures

Version 1.0   September 21, 2011

Michael Shallcross
Nancy Deromedi

Bentley Historical Library
Digital Curation Division

Table of Contents

Introduction

Quality assurance (QA) refers to the systematic evaluation of an activity or product "to maximize the probability that minimum standards of quality are being attained."[1] In performing QA on websites preserved by the University Archives and Records Program (UARP) and Michigan Historical Collections (MHC), the Bentley Historical Library (BHL) seeks to ensure the accuracy and integrity of its web archives collections.

BHL staff involved in the preservation and QA of archived websites should have a some understanding of the design and architecture of websites (including links, embedded content, web forms, navigational menus, etc.) as well as basic knowledge of HTML, Cascading Style Sheets (CSS), JavaScript (JS), and other significant web page features. A familiarity with the curatorial interface and basic functions of the California Digital Library (CDL)'s Web Archiving Service (WAS) is also important.

During this process, a BHL QA specialist will:

- Identify incomplete, inaccurate, or unsuccessful web captures
- Determine the underlying causes or issues that led to the substandard captures. This step may require the QA specialist to:
  o Verify crawl settings
  o Review crawl reports and logs
  o Inspect the content, layout, features, and source code of the target site
- Document:
  o Any technical limitations, robots.txt exclusions, or other issues that may have prevented a faithful and accurate capture of a website.
  o Contact information for webmasters (if necessary)
  o Recommendations to delete captures or initiate new crawls

Given the inherent challenges of various content types and the technical limitations of the WAS infrastructure, it is not feasible to perfectly preserve the content, appearance, functionality, and structure of all targeted websites. Although QA may not resolve all issues with a given archived website, careful documentation will help to establish the provenance of content and record actions taken by the archives. Information gathered during QA will also enable the library to revisit problematic captures as web archiving technology continues to mature.

The CDL's release of additional quality assurance tools and reporting features for WAS in late May/early June 2011 will require the revision of these guidelines and procedures. This document will also be reviewed on an annual basis to ensure that the information and procedures contained herein are current and applicable.

---

[1] "Quality assurance." *Wikipedia* (May 5, 2011). Retrieved on May 6, 2011 from http://en.wikipedia.org/wiki/Quality_assurance.

2   9/21/2011

QA Procedures for Bentley Historical Library Web Archives

1. For each site, use the QA Spreadsheet to record:

    a. Your initials

    b. The date on which QA was conducted

    c. The number of captures currently held for the site

    d. The date range of the captures (may be a single date).

2. From the "Manage Sites" screen of the WAS curatorial interface, click on the site name to access the "Site Summary." (You may choose to right-click and open in a new tab.)

    a. Capture Settings

        i. Verify that the site name (i.e. "Department of Chemistry Web Archives (University of Michigan)") adheres to BHL conventions.

            1. BHL conventions for site titles may be found in the document: "Bentley Historical Library Web Archives: Methodology for the Acquisition of Content" (pp. 3-4).

            2. Modify site names as needed in step 8 (being sure to respect the original site's name, if possible).

        ii. Check if "linked pages" are being captured:

            1. For U of M content:

                a. Only "high priority" sites should include the capture of linked pages.

                b. For all other sites, linked pages should not be captured to avoid an excessive amount of content in the web archives.

            2. For MHC content, the QA specialist may need to verify if linked content should be captured. (See later steps.)

    b. Scheduling

        i. For U of M:

1. Only "high priority" sites will be scheduled for more than one capture a year (see list on p. 7).

2. Campus event websites (including the Arts Portal, Online Event calendar, etc.) and the Gateway may also be captured more frequently.

3. All other sites should only be captured on an annual basis.

   ii. For MHC:

1. If there are multiple captures scheduled, conduct crawl comparisons to see if these are necessary.

2. Check with Project Administrators before adjusting schedule.

  c. Descriptive Data

   i. Check Description, Creator, Publisher, Subjects, and Geographic coverage elements to ensure that they follow BHL conventions.

1. BHL conventions for metadata entry may be found in the document: "Bentley Historical Library Web Archives: Methodology for the Acquisition of Content" (pp. 7-8).

2. Edit metadata as needed in step 8.

   ii. Check "Site Tags" (on right hand side)to see if the archived website could be grouped with other relevant subjects. (This determination may require the QA Specialist to view the archived page.)

1. A full listing of tags for a specific project is available under the "Administration > Mange Tags" menu item.

2. BHL conventions for tagging may be found in the document: "Bentley Historical Library Web Archives: Methodology for the Acquisition of Content" (p. 9).

3. Only Project Administrators may add new tags to the current list. Please inform the appropriate administrator

9   9/21/2011

if you believe that an additional tag (or tags) may be
necessary.

    d. Capture History

        i. Check general the following for potential issues:

            1. "Status": may reveal ongoing technical issues

            2. "Files": could be problematic if extremely low or high

            3. "Duration": could be problematic if extremely short or
timed out

3. Click "View Results" link to access the Crawl Overview

    a. Check seed URL(s) for redirects

    b. In case of an extremely small number of files or short duration, check
"Robot Exclusions" statistics to see if the crawler was blocked

    c. In case of an extremely large number of files or in the event that the
crawler exceeded the 36 hour duration, check the "Hosts Report" to see
how many URLs are remaining for the main seed URL(s)

    d. Pending the review of the archived content, it may be necessary to
examine other crawl reports.

4. View archived website

    a. Verify that content is an archived resource (instead of a redirected 'live'
web page).

    b. Verify that CSS files are present (i.e. pages are *not* text only)

    c. Click on main navigational links (depending upon crawl settings,
additional content may or may not have been intended for capture).

    d. For high priority targets, click through the entire site to ensure that
significant content and features have been captured.

    e. Troubleshooting:

        i. If a particular resource does not appear in the archive, conduct a
search for the URL (search feature available from the main
Results screen)

      ii. Viewing the source code of the original page will help to identify web design features or resources that may not have been captured.

      iii. Check live version of archived site (if available) to compare appearance of archived version.

      iv. Check reports/crawl logs to understand issues with the crawl.

         1. Look up specific URLs to see if they were captured.

         2. Trace progress of crawl, identify where issues arose.

  f. If (for MHC or high priority U of M sites) linked pages have been captured, determine if these contain significant information. This may require consulting the "Hosts" report (or others).

5. For sites with multiple captures:

  a. If there are more than 3 captures, only review a sample (i.e. the first, one in the middle, and the most recent).

  b. Check to see if content/features change significantly between captures. Are these frequent captures necessary? Does older content (such as course schedules or news stories) tend to stay on the site as it is updated? Will a less-frequent capture schedule allow us to preserve the same information?

6. If there is a notable problem with the crawl, identify the underlying cause and document the issue on the QA spreadsheet.

  a. Robots.txt exclusions

  b. Crawl limits (timed out)

  c. Display errors:

  d. Seed redirect

  e. 'Live links'—rendering error

  f. Missing .css files

  g. Resources not in archive (partial)

  h. Seed issues: did not capture (at all)

11   9/21/2011

      i. Crawl of unusual size

      j. Adjust crawl frequency

7. Make recommendations on the QA Spreadsheet in regards to:

    a. Back up spreadsheet while working on it

    b. The deletion of a previous crawl.

        i. Deletions should be reserved for crawls that were misdirected, erroneous, or never completed (due to robots.txt or technical issues).

        ii. In some cases, excessively large captures (i.e. greater than 4 GB) may need to be deleted to preserve space.

    c. The initiation of a new crawl.

    d. Reducing the crawl frequency of high-priority sites

    e. Communication with the contact owner if it will be necessary to request a modification of the robots.txt file or resolve another issue with the site. Try to identify and record the name/email address of the site's webmaster or main contact.

8. Edit crawl settings:

    a. "Capture Linked Pages"

        i. For U of M content:

            1. Only "high priority" sites should include the capture of linked pages.

            2. For all other sites, the capture linked pages setting should be changed to "**No**" to avoid an excessive amount of content in the web archives.

        ii. For MHC content, the QA specialist may need to

    b. If you determine that the web archives need to capture a smaller/wider range of content, make one (or more) of the following changes (and note in the QA Spreadsheet):

        i. Decrease/increase scope (host, directory, or page)

12   9/21/2011

ii. Decrease/increase maximum crawl time (1 or 36 hours)

iii. Recommend the deletion/addition of additional seed URLs on the QA Spreadsheet.

c. While crawl schedules should be accurately set at the time of capture, check with an archivist if the frequency for a site seems too low/high.

Common Issues and Problems with Web Captures

- Crawler traps: These are essentially infinite loops from which a robot is unable to escape. Online calendars are among the most common examples. The crawler will start with the present date and capture page after page of the calendar until the crawl expires without preserving more meaningful site content. The resulting capture may have a very large number of files and will likely reach the maximum time setting before finishing.

- Unexpected seed redirects: The web crawler may be unexpectedly redirected from the target seed URL and begin the crawl on a random page (sometimes completely unassociated with the original seed URL). The redirection may truncate the crawl, cause important content (such as a home page) to be missed, or may lead to a crawler trap.

- Inaccurate seed URLs: Some sites require the crawler to start at a specific web page instead of a basic domain name. For instance, the accurate capture of the U of M Law School required http://www.law.umich.edu/Pages/default.aspx to be included as a seed (instead of just http://www.law.umich.edu/). Other sites will require the crawler to start at ".../home" or ".../index.html." Failure to include accurate seeds may result in a failed crawl, unexpected redirect, or a crawler trap. The BHL QA specialist may need to visit the live website to identify the exact URL from which the crawler should begin.

- Robots.txt files: A "robots.txt" file is an Internet convention used by webmasters to prevent all or certain sections of websites from being captured by a web crawler. The robots.txt must reside in the root of the site's domain and its presence may be verified by typing '/robots.txt' after the root URL (i.e. http://umich.edu/robots.txt). By convention, a web crawler or robot will read the robots.txt file of a target site before doing anything else. This text file will specify what sections of a site the robot is forbidden to crawl. A typical robots.txt exclusion statement is as follows:
  > User-agent: *
  > Disallow: /

  User-agent' refers to the crawler; * is a wildcard symbol that indicates the exclusion applies to all robots; and / applies the exclusion to all pages on the

13   9/21/2011

DRAFT

How to Accession Electronic Records to the Spartan Archive Storage Vault

1. Receive transfer from unit, including transmittal form and inventory

2. Create Archivists' Toolkit record
   - Assign 'A' accession #
   - Enter accession date (indicates accession created)
   - Link to Resource (MSU unit/record group)

3. Provide accession # to unit

4. Add accession # to transmittal form

5. If transmittal form and inventory are paper, scan as PDFs. If transmittal form and inventory are digital files, print a copy.

6. File paper version of transmittal form in records management files. Inventory should be stapled to transmittal form, if available.

7. If necessary, create a folder in the Storage Vault for the record group. The name of the folder for the record group should be the official UAHC record group number.

For electronic records coming in on hard drives or removable media:

8. Label hard drive or media with accession #. If more than one piece of hardware or media is in the accession, label each with the accession # plus a sequential number. For example, Axxxxxx-1, Axxxxxx-2, etc.

9. Write protect hard drive or media, if possible.

10. Connect hard drive or insert media on electronic records processing workstation.

11. Check for viruses on hard drive or media using the Kaspersky virus scanning utility.
    - Connect hard drive or insert removable media as necessary
    - Open Kaspersky.
    - Select disk to scan.
    - Click "Start Scan" button.
    - If viruses are present, Kaspersky will identify the infected files and ask to quarantine them. Agree to quarantine. (Steps in this case TBD.)

3/15/12

DRAFT

12. Accession files on hard drive or media into the Digital Shelf using Duke Data Accessioner.
   - Open Duke Data Accessioner
   - Under "Adapters" menu, select DROID and JHOVE adapters.
   - Under "Metadata Managers, select Duke PREMIS.
   - Enter your name, the accession number assigned, and the collection number.
   - Click the button labeled "Accession Directory" and select the accession's record group folder in the Storage Vault.
   - Click the disk icon and select the drive or media to be accessioned.
   - Ensure that a logical name is entered into the Disk Name text box. For example, if the accession includes several CDs, the first might be named CD-1, the second CD-2, and so on.
   - Click the "Disk Label" tab. Transcribe any appropriate label text into the box.
   - Click on the "Additional Notes" tab and enter any pertinent information that a processor might need to know about the original disk or the data. For example, file formats found of the preserved files. Any restrictions could be noted here as well.
   - Click the "Migrate" button. This will create a folder labeled with the accession number in the record group folder. The new folder will contain a folder labeled with the assigned disk name containing two files: (1) the contents of the media and (2) an XML file that includes checksums, creation dates, and other metadata for the files on the media.
   - Verify the creation of the new folder and files in the record group folder.
   - Repeat the steps above for each hard drive or media in the accession. Each addition to the accession will result in a new folder containing the contents of that media. Additional XML markup will concatenate in the original XML file.
   - For more on using the Duke Data Accessioner, refer to the Duke University Data Accessioner guide, http://www.duke.edu/~ses44/downloads/guide.pdf.

13. Remove media. Place all media related to the accession in a folder/envelope labeled with date of accession and accession number and store in the electronic records accession file drawer.

14. What to do with hard drive? (TBD)

15. Complete accession record in Archivists' Toolkit
   - Title – Unit ID, Unit Name
   - Extent—in GB
   - Summary (if needed)
   - Date range
   - Location—R Drive and/or Digital Accessions Drawer (for original media)
   - Retention Rule ("Permanent")
   - Description of records. Include information about transfer mechanism, original media, and any viruses in original transfer, if applicable.
   - Link to external document (transmittal form). Use inventory field only if needed

3/15/12

3. University of Virginia: Cheuse Papers Processing Plan

University of Virginia
Processing Plan
Collection 10726, The Papers of Alan Cheuse

Collection Name:	The Papers of Alan Cheuse
Collection Date:	Ca. 1950 – 2009
Collection Number:	10726; accessions _ through al
Extent (pre-processing):	83 disks (3.5" and CD) approx. 5.31 MB; ca. 80 linear feet
Types of materials:	3.5" disks and CDs, video cassettes and DVDs, paper manuscripts
Custodial History:	Alan Cheuse placed the papers on loan to the Library beginning in 1987. Earlier accessions were then purchased in 2003 with a commitment to purchase further groups.
Restrictions from Donors:	Explicit digital rights have yet been discussed. Four series (Accessions 17, 18, 20, and 21) are restricted from access until 2012.
Separated Materials:	Disks have been separated from the manuscript drafts and are stored with the other media and a/v.
Related Materials:	None
Preservation Concerns:	None
Languages other than English:	None
Overview of Contents:	This collection consists of the papers of the American author, book reviewer, and George Mason University professor, Alan Cheuse. These papers include manuscripts for articles, speeches, interviews, and short stories; book reviews; screen plays; cassette tape recordings; computer disks; video cassette & DVD; printed material; contracts and royalties; passports; photographs and drawings; correspondence; research material; short stories by other authors; appointment calendars; short stories and book manuscripts.
Existing Order and description:	Sixteen of the thirty-two accessions have been processed separately, as per institutional practices. They are described in both EAD finding aids and MARC records. They are each organized by type of writing (correspondence, topical files, novel manuscripts, review manuscripts, etc.) to the folder level. The other 16 accessions are recorded in MARC records at varying degrees of detail, some with no more than a title, date, and generic note. All computer media has been separated, numbered, and is referenced in finding aids and records, but has mostly not been processed. The contents of some disks were printed and filed with paper manuscripts. Seven of the accessions contain computer disk materials. Only one of these accessions has been described in an EAD finding aid.

AIMS: An Inter-Institutional Model for Stewardship

Desired Processing:	All computer media should be processed. Additionally, all accessions should be combined into a single finding aid. Where EAD exists, these records will be combined into a single <archdesc> and <dsc> with each accession being represented as a series. The accessions represented by MARC records will be converted to series components. In addition, subject headings, which were not included in the original EAD, should be added from all MARC records.
	No further work will be done with paper materials at this time.
	The processor will create disk images of the disks and then process using FTK. Disks containing commercial works that were used for research purposes should not be imaged or stored at this time. Individual files will be labeled with the disk number so that they may later be associated with the correct container element in the EAD. Titles of individual works will be added to the finding aid so that some reference to the works available on the disks is present. This is to match the level of processing of the paper manuscripts, which are indicated by name within the collection descriptions.
	Files containing confidential information will be completely restricted at this time. Obsolete file formats will not be migrated at this time, but this work should be considered in the future. Access to materials on the disk will be at the individual file level. After imaging the disk a copy of the image will be transferred to the StoreNext preservation store. Copies of the unrestricted files will be added to the Hypatia repository for public access.
	The disk images will be referenced by identifier number within the ead. They will exist as individual subcomponents of the accession or sub-series (if it exists) and the disk number will be referenced in a "unitid" attribute. The finalized finding aid will also be uploaded into the Hypatia repository and the individual files will be linked to the accession or container they belong to.
Next steps	Reprocessing all accessions into one collection arranged intellectually, rather than intellectually within individual accessions, is recommended for the future when the collection is deemed "complete." As technology and infrastructure develop, migration of obsolete formats and redaction within restricted files in order to make them available should also be undertaken.
Notes to Processors:	Examine the contents of the CDs later in the series to determine which are simply copies of commercially produced works and do not need to be imaged.
Anticipated Time for Processing:	5 days

AIMS: An Inter-Institutional Model for Stewardship

4. Yale University: Tobin Collection Processing Plan

Processing Work Plan

Institution: MSSA
Archivist: Mark A. Matienzo
Date: June 7, 2011
Collection title: James Tobin papers
Creator: Tobin, James
Current call number(s): MS 1746, **Accession 2004-M-088**
Provenance: Gift of Elizabeth Tobin, 2004.
Extent: 8.75 linear feet; 27 3.5" inch diskettes (35.7 MB)

Overview:

Research strengths: correspondence regarding professional activities; working and final drafts of conference papers, periodical columns, and other publications.

Types of electronic records present: Correspondence (e-mail and computer-written letters); writings; spreadsheets and graphs; office files (biographical statements, calendars, publication lists, etc.), course materials. Files are primarily WordPerfect and Lotus 1-2-3; some Quicken files exist; e-mail is in text form, either in Eudora mailboxes individually saved text files.

Significant preservation concerns: See file formats above. Most significant concern is Lotus 1-2-3 files; several should be considered compound objects with graphs and formatting information.

Description:

Current: Minimal. Labels from individual diskettes have been transcribed as component titles within finding aid.

Proposed enhancement: Description should follow executed organization as specified below.

Recommended description work for later: see under organization.

Organization:

Current: Hard to determine. Paper records do not seem to have a coherent overall organization, with the exception of the correspondence; however, correspondence is still scattered between "Letters to Jim," "Professional Correspondence", "Nobel Prize Correspondence," and "Personal Correspondence." Writings are very disorganized;

Diskettes appear to be used as transfer media for files between his office, his home, and his cottage in Wisconsin. A few disks, or sets thereof, show some grouping based on type of records, such as "office files" (publication lists, telephone lists/address books) and letters that Tobin wrote in WordPerfect. Writings are not grouped together thematically.

Proposed arrangement: Arrangement should be based on record types. Within the electronic records for this accession, logical groupings and subgroupings are as follows:

- Correspondence, 1992-2001 and undated
    - Correspondence written using WordPerfect, 1992-2000
    - E-mail, 1996-2001 and undated
- Course materials for Economics 480B, 1998
    - Lotus 1-2-3 spreadsheets, 1992-1997

Appendix E: Sample Processing Plans

11

- o "Primer" spreadsheets and graphs, 1996-1997
- Office files, 1995-2001
    - o Biographical statements
    - o Calendars
    - o Lists of Tobin's publications
    - o Quicken files
    - o Recommendation letters and lists of recommendations
    - o Telephone lists
- Writings, 1992-2001

Of all groupings, the Writings grouping would need the most considerable organization and description. In the short term I recommend either not listing individual files, or listing individual files with filename and date only.

Recommended arrangement work for later: Combine paper records and electronic records into a common arrangement. Considerable attention to Tobin's personal papers is needed, especially those related to his military service. Arrange writings alphabetically by title, identify explicit drafts, and reconcile against publication lists included in this accession as available from the Cowles Foundation. In the long term, we should plan to process the collection as a whole and integrate all the accessions into a common arrangement.

Appraisal:

Diskettes 1-3, 11, and 17 should be discarded; #1-3 contain printer drivers; #11 contains modem software; and #17 contains many deleted files and is mostly blank.

Some of Tobin's "office files" are of uncertain or low research value, such as the Quicken files, biographical statements and telephone lists. The publication lists are of questionable value as the Cowles Foundation has a detailed publication list in PDF form; however, Tobin has some topic-specific publication lists that may be helpful. Some of the office files also appear to be inventories of paper files, which may or may not be reflected in the paper records previously acquired.

Restrictions:

Other (paper) correspondence within this accession is restricted. E-mail contains both personal and professional correspondence; personal/family correspondence includes reference to health issues. Consider restricting e-mail under similar conditions. Most letters written using WordPerfect are professional in nature. Recommendation letters and Quicken files (which deal with Tobin's personal finances) should be restricted.

Preservation:

Proposed action now: Investigate migration options for Lotus 1-2-3 files, particularly those that reference graphs.

Recommended for later: Migrate WordPerfect files to PDF/A; migrate e-mail to a different format.

Access:

See Preservation. Files should be extracted into a storage option such as the YUL Rescue Repository so they can be paged on request. This collections does not have a high level use, so there is probably not an immediate need to create use copies.

Beinecke Rare Book & Manuscript Unit, Manuscript Unit, Processing Manual section on Electronic Files

5.6 Electronic Files

Computer media containing electronic or born digital files are sometimes found in manuscript collections and, like other collection material, should be accounted for in the arrangement and description of the archive.

Disks and other media are logged and pulled when a collection is accessioned and acknowledged in the AT Accession module. The content is captured for preservation, appraisal, and access, and the original media is returned to the collection and placed in Restricted Fragile Papers.

5.6.1 Security & Access

MS Unit and selected Beinecke staff members have access to use copies of disk images on a YU network directory.

Library guidelines for research use of eletronic files in manuscript collections are posted on the Beinecke website under Research Services at Ordering Copies / Photographs / Scans.

5.6.2 Collection Development

Library guidelines for collecting born digital manuscript material are maintained on the network directory under Curatorial\YCAL\Born Digital Docs.

5.6.3 Accessioning

Accessioning of computer media is defined by the library as capture of the content off the source media. Computer media should be removed from manuscript collections upon receipt or during baseline processing of new accessions in order to be

YALE UNIVERSITY

Beinecke Rare Book & Manuscript Unit, Processing Manual. Electronic Files

accessioned. The Manuscript Unit pursues a strategy of bit-level capture through disk imaging.

Documentation on the accessioning (i.e. disk imaging) of each piece of media is captured on an "Electronic Records Media Log". The logs are maintained by accession number on the department's Accessioning webpages at https://collaborate.library.yale.edu/BeineckeLibrary/MsUnit/accessioning/Lists/Electronic%20Records%20Media%20Log/AllItems.aspx.

Additional documentation on the "Electronic Files Workflow for New Accessions" and "Electronic File Log" can be found on the department's Accessioning webpages.

5.6.4 Appraisal

There are tools for appraising/analyzing content on disk images and electronic files. For appraising or analyzing content of files in disk images, commercial forensic tools (FTK Imager and AccessData FTK) are available. Consult the appropriate staff member regarding use of these tools in planning for processing. For appraising/analyzing the content of electronic files, the library has file viewing software (Quick View Plus) on some staff workstations, public workstations, and laptops. See the Quick View Plus website for comprehensive list of file types supported by the current version of the viewer.

5.6.5 Intellectual Arrangement

General note

When computer media is found in a collection it should be routed into the computer media accessioning workflow--see step 2 of the "Electronic Files Workflow for New Accessions".

YALE UNIVERSITY

Beinecke Rare Book & Manuscript Unit, Processing Manual. Electronic Files

When we receive computer media for which we have the technical infrastructure in place in the digital preservation lab to accession it, we will attempt to accession it in time for staff working on the paper component of the collection to analyze the records contained on the media and possibly integrate them into the collection. This will depend on various factors, including the volume of media in the accession and staff availability. This may enable staff to complete processing for some collections.

Because baseline processing of new accessions was implemented prior to disk imaging, collections dating from roughly 2008-2011 were processed before the policy above was in place. The result in most cases is that media was routed into the computer media accessioning workflow and documented in the finding aid only (as media and not records) in Restricted Fragile Papers. This represents a group of collections for which additional processing should be done in order to integrate the born digital content.

In baseline processing, staff should first consult the accessioning and baseline project documentation to determine if selected projects contain computer media. In the ACQ record, see the TTL, MAT, and LNO fields, and in the backlog files, see the Notes field. If collections contain computer media, staff should then consult the "Electronic Records Media Log" documenting accessions and/or contact the appropriate staff person to determine if the computer media has been fully accessioned and the records can be appraised/analyzed. If born digital materials are ready for processing, staff can consult about documentation, tools, and strategies.

5.6.5.1 Computer Disks

Most electronic files in manuscript collections accessioned before 2008 came on the standard data storage devices in use since the mid 1970s: 5 ¼ and 3 ½ inch disks, zip disks, and compact discs (CDs). When evaluating files on these media formats, the following instructions may best apply.

The number of disks and electronic files in a collection may determine whether you can conduct item-level analysis. Most files on these media formats include drafts of writings or material relating to writing projects and correspondence (in word processing formats). When possible, respect context and original order in arrangement. When original order cannot be established, in general, small numbers of disks and files lend themselves to item or file-level analysis and arrangement by content. With larger numbers of disks and files, and disks with mixed files (e.g. writings, correspondence, etc.), other factors will probably also need to to considered in order to determine whether to arrange material by content or format. In baseline processing, media may also be listed where found (disks should be housed in Restricted Fragile).

As of December 2011, several collections containing computer media have been processed to varying levels, providing us with some useful examples:

For an example of a hybrid collection in which the electronic and paper materials were fully integrated and arranged to the file/item level, see the James Welch Papers (YCAL MSS 248).

For a baseline processing project example of a collection containing a moderate number of disks (33) in which some analysis of the content allowed the born digital and paper material to be integrated and arranged at the file level, see the Caryl Phillips Papers (GEN MSS 793).

For a baseline project example of a collection containing a smaller number of disks (22) in which context alone allowed for arrangement at the subseries/file level, see the Howard Roberts Lamar Papers (WA MSS S-2639).

For an example of a collection in which the electronic files were arranged by format, see the George Whitmore Papers (YCAL MSS 274).

One way to keep track of electronic files when doing item-level arrangement is to create a dummy folder, labeled with information about the file, and incorporate the folder into the sorting of like material. For example, when arranging material for a particular title in a writing series, place a dummy folder for an electronic draft (see "Hotel Christobel" example in section 5.6.7.6) in the sequence of materials relating to the title.

Other types of text files can be treated the same way, placing them in the appropriate intellectual and sequential location of related files.

5.6.5.2 Snapshot Accessions, Computers, External Hard-drives

When dealing with digital records acquired directly from record creators through snapshot accessions or on retired media, such as computers (and possibly external hard drives), respect context and original order as recommended in the "Paradigm Exemplars for Arrangment," *Workbook of Digital Private Papers*, available at http://www.paradigm.ac.uk/workbook/cataloguing/ead-exemplars.html.

5.6.5.3 Special Cases

Some electronic files may not lend themselves to the management and access strategies outlined above. In these cases, other strategies may be desirable or necessary to provide staff and research access to the files.

For difficult-to-access files, files prone to corruption, and relational files, it might be preferable to print a copy of the file, rather than rely on the electronic copy, for reference and research use. These copies would go into the archival boxes just as Preservation Photocopies do, and would be clearly marked as printouts from electronic files.

For relational files, such as databases and hyperlinked documents, it may be better to recreate a mini-environment with the original software. For example, a suite of web pages could be copied to a folder that also contains a simple version of an HTML browser. Or a database file could be coupled with a viewing version of the database program.

For graphic files, Quick View Plus and other file viewers can open and display most types of images formats. Dynamic image data (e.g., motion picture files), however, will need to be viewed on software that can properly sequence them.

For batch files that we might describe at a finer level (e.g. Eudora e-mail folders containing e-mail from numerous correspondents, accessible in the original Eudora software), the access methods could take two forms: Arrange the file at the end of the Correspondence series as a general correspondence file (e.g. "Work Letters 1997") and include important names in a note. Use the original software, if available, to access the individual components, print them out, and file them as you would paper-based correspondence. Printouts must be marked to show that they are copies of material received in electronic form.

5.6.6 Physical Arrangement

Computer media should be placed in Restricted Fragile.

5.6.7 Description

In the finding aid, the existence, quantity, technical specifications and requirements, and conservation relating to computer media and electronic files can be described in the following EAD elements: Physical Description, Description of the Papers, Information About Access, and Notes.

5.6.7.1 Physical Description <extent>

The extent of computer media and/or electronic files may be documented at the collection, series/accesion, and folder level as appropriate.

When a collection or series/accession consists solely of digital records, record extent in terms of file storage size and, in some cases, number of files. Though *DACS* does not offer an example of digital extent recorded in terms of size, the general rule at 2.5.3

YALE UNIVERSITY

Beinecke Rare Book & Manuscript Unit, Processing Manual. Electronic Files

seems to allow for it. See also *RAD* 9.5B2, *ISAD(G)* 3.1.5 and the Paradigm fonds-level description recommendations, available at http://www.paradigm.ac.uk/workbook/cataloguing/ead-fonds.html. As of April 2010, recent professional practice and recommendations indicate use of gigabytes and megabytes. That said, use the most appropriate file storage size per *RAD* 9.5B2. For example:

Physical Description: 3.71 megabytes

In accordance with *DACS* 2.5.7, extent may be further defined through a parallel statement. This could be used to record a large number of files. For example:

Physical Description: 227 megabytes (2,215 files)

Alternately, when the file storage size is not available, describe the quantity in terms of material type(s) in accordance with *DACS* 2.5.5. See also *RAD* 9.5B3. This will be the case when some or all formats are unreadable or, in baseline processing, if media has not yet been fully accessioned. For example:

Physical Description: 57 computer disks

Similarly, in baseline processing, when the file storage size is not yet available, qualify the statement to highlight the existence of the material type in accordance with *DACS* 2.5.6. For example:

Physical Description: 7 folders, including 3 computer disks

EAD allows for multiples statements of extent. When the digital records make up a significant part of a hybrid collection or series/accession, provide two parallel expressions of extent, one for the physical content and one for the digital content. For example:

Physical Description: 4.17' (10 boxes)

Physical Description: 227 megabytes (2,215 files)

5.6.7.2 Description of the Papers <scopecontent>

The existence of computer media or electronic files can be noted in the Description of the Papers. Otherwise, if electronic files are arranged at the series level, this can be discussed in the series scope and content note.

If electronic files have been printed out, rather than left in electronic form, this should be noted. If they have been printed out because the electronic file was damaged or otherwise problematic, be sure to note that the file was "salvaged" from the electronic version. If some files are printed out and others are left in electronic form, provide the rationale for this decision.

5.6.7.3 Information about Access <accessrestrict> and <phystech>

Access restrictions on original media and files should be noted in the Access Restrict element in accordance with *DACS* 4.2. Use the following format: [Container type] [number or span] ([type of media]): Restricted Fragile Material. Reference copies [may be requested/are available]. Consult Access Services for further information. For example:

Box 4 (computer disks): Restricted Fragile Material. Reference copies of electronic files may be requested. Consult Access Services for further information.

Box 14 (laptop computer): Restricted Fragile Material. Reference copies of electronic files are available. Consult Access Services for further information.

Technical requirements for patron access to copies are meant to be noted in the Physical Characteristics/Technical Requirements element in accordance with *DACS* 4.3.5 but, because the this element is rarely used in YUL finding aids, this information will be added to the access restriction in the Access Restrict element if appropriate.

5.6.7.4 Notes <notes>

Preservation actions that results in changes to the file, such as migration, should be documented in a note element in accordance with *DACS* 7.1.4 See also *RAD* 9.8B10b. For example:

> Electronic files migrated by National Data Conversion from the original word-processing software (WordStar for CP/M) to Wordstar 4.0 for DOS and to ASCII to maintain readability of data. Technical specifications are filed with media in Restricted Fragile.

Expanding on *DACS* 7.1.4, in an effort to be more transparent about the reproduction process, document refreshment or ingest into the local digital repository. For example:

Electronic files migrated by National Data Conversion from the original word-processing software (WordStar for CP/M) to Wordstar 4.0 for DOS and to ASCII to maintain readability of data. Wordstar 4.0 for DOS and ASCII files refreshed into the Yale University Library Rescue Repository. Technical specifications are filed with media in Restricted Fragile.

5.6.7.5 Series and Subseries Headings

Local practice is to apply the term "Electronic Files" to series and subseries headings. Electronic Files is preferred to Computer Files, the *AACR2* GMD (*AACR2* 1.1C1), as a broader and ostensibly more accurate term, one, for example, that can encompass electronic or born-digital files created on contemporary portable devices (such as digital cameras, cell phones, PDAs, etc.) not commonly identified as computers. Electronic Files is preferred to Electronic Records in order to distinguish materials created or received by individuals common to personal papers from records created or received in the course of institutional activity. Electronic is also preferred to Digital as a broader term, encompassing both analog and digital formats.

YALE UNIVERSITY

Beinecke Rare Book & Manuscript Unit, Processing Manual. Electronic Files

At this time Beinecke does not apply headings by specific format (e.g. text files, image files).

See George Whitmore Papers (YCAL MSS 274).

5.6.7.6 Folder Headings and Folder Notes

The recommended chief source of information for electronic files is the title screen (*AACR2* 9.0B1). Transcribe the title screen of the file when applying item-level analysis and arrangement. Other prescribed sources of information include the physical carriers or labels. When applying disk-level analysis, transcribe information from the physical carrier (e.g. disk or jewel case) or label. See the George Whitmore Papers (YCAL MSS 274).

When transcribing or supplying folder headings for files arranged at the item level, such as a draft, add the term "electronic," as you would the GMD. When electronic files are arranged intellectually, outside of an "Electronic Files" series/accession, always include the following folder note in an Access Restrict element <accessrestrict> in accordance with *DACS 4.2*:

Computer disks are restricted. Copies of electronic files may be requested through Access Services:[Accession #, Disk #, Disk label]

For example:

Series I. Writings

PLAYS

"Hotel Christobel"

4 21 Research notes   1990

22   Preliminary sketches   1990 Oct 1

          Draft, electronic   1990 Nov

                Computer disks are restricted. Copies of electronic files may be
                requested through Access Services: [Accessions #],
                Disk#17, Hotel.doc

23   Galley proof   1990 Dec

See James Welch Papers (YCAL MSS 248).

Item-level description might also include the original file format.

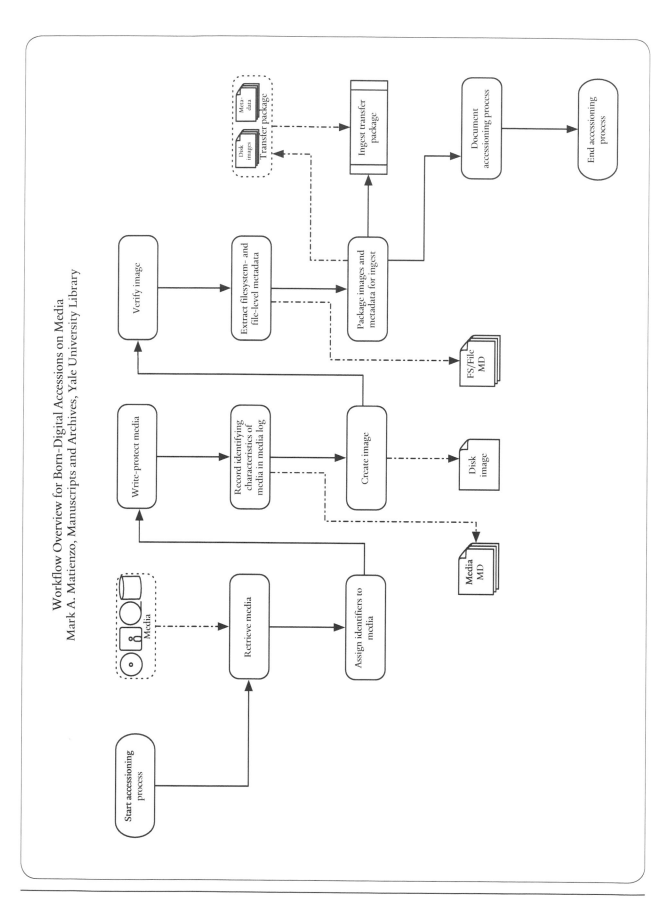

Workflow Overview for Born-Digital Accessions on Media
Mark A. Matienzo, Manuscripts and Archives, Yale University Library

SELECTED RESOURCES

Journal Articles and Other Works

AIMS Working Group. 2012. *AIMS Born-Digital Collections: An Inter-Institutional Model for Stewardship.* http://www2.lib.virginia.edu/aims/whitepaper/AIMS_final_text.pdf

Authenticity Task Force. "Appendix 2: Requirements for Assessing and Maintaining the Authenticity of Electronic Records." In *The Long-Term Preservation of Authentic Electronic Records: Findings of the InterPARES Project,* by the International Research on Permanent Authentic Records in Electronic Systems (InterPARES Project), March 2002. http://www.interpares.org/book/interpares_book_k_app02.pdf

Bentley Historical Library. "Sustainable Formats and Conversion Strategies at the Bentley Historical Library." November 9, 2011. http://bentley.umich.edu/dchome/resources/BHL_PreservationStrategies_v01.pdf

Bradley, Kevin. "Defining Digital Sustainability." *Library Trends* 56, no.1 (2007): 148–63.

Carroll, Laura, Erika Farr, Peter Hornsby, and Ben Ranker. "A Comprehensive Approach to Born-Digital Archives." *Archivaria* 72 (Fall 2011): 61–92.

City of Vanvouver Archives. "City of Vanvouver Digital Archives System Workflow v.1 (Fall 2010)." http://artefactual.com/wiki/images/4/40/COV_Digital_Archives_System_Workflow_v1.pdf

Cunningham, Adrian. "Good Digital Records Don't Just 'Happen': Embedding Recordkeeping as an Organic Component of Business Processes and Systems." *Archivaria* 71 (Spring 2011): 21–34.

Davis, Susan E. "Electronic Records Planning in 'Collecting' Repositories." *American Archivist* 71 (Spring/Summer 2008): 167–89.

Dooley, Jackie, and Katherine Luce. *Taking Our Pulse: The OCLC Research Survey of Special Collections and Archives.* Dublin, OH: OCLC Research, 2010. http://www.oclc.org/research/publications/library/2010/2010-11.pdf

Dow, Elizabeth H. *Electronic Records in the Manuscript Repository.* Lanham, Maryland: Scarecrow Press, 2009.

Erway, Ricky. "Defining 'Born Digital'." OCLC Research, November 2010. www.oclc.org/research/activities/hiddencollections/borndigital.pdf

Ferguson-Boucher, Kirsten, and Nicole Convery. "Storing Information in the Cloud—A Research Project." *Journal of the Society of Archivists* 32, no. 2 (October 2011): 221–39.

Forstrom, Michael. "Managing Electronic Records in Manuscript Collections: A Case Study from the Beinecke Rare Book and Manuscript Library." *American Archivist* 72, no. 2 (2009): 460–77.

Fyffe, Richard, Deborah Ludwig, and Beth Forrest Warner. "Digital Preservation in Action: Toward a Campus-wide Program." Research Bulletin, Vol. 2005, Issue 19, September 13, 2005. Boulder, CO: EDUCAUSE Center for Applied Research, 2005. http://net.educause.edu/ir/library/pdf/ERB0519.pdf

Gehring, Cynthia, Judith Borreson Caruso, and David A. Gift. "Electronic Records Management: Today's High Stakes." Research Bulletin 8, 2010. Boulder, CO: EDUCAUSE Center for Applied Research, 2010. http://net.educause.edu/ir/library/pdf/ERB1008.pdf

Goldman, Ben. "Bridging the Gap: Taking Practical Steps Toward Managing Born-Digital Collections in Manuscript Repositories." *RBM: A Journal of Rare Books, Manuscripts, and Cultural Heritage* 12, no. 1 (Spring 2011): 11–24. http://rbm.acrl.org/content/12/1/11.full.pdf+html

Keough, Brian, and Mark Wolfe. "Moving the Archivist Closer to the Creator: Implementing Integrated Archival Policies for Born Digital Photography at Colleges and Universities." *Journal of Archival Organization* 10, no. 1 (2012): 69–83.

Kiehne, Thomas, Vivian Spoliansky, and Catherine Stollar, "From Floppies to Repository: A Transition of Bits." A Case Study in Preserving the Michael Joyce Digital Papers at the Harry Ransom Center. May 2005. https://pacer.ischool.utexas.edu/handle/2081/941

Kirschenbaum, Matthew, Richard Ovendon, and Gabriela Redwine. *Digital Forensics and Born-Digital Content in Cultural Heritage Collections*. Washington, DC: Council on Library and Information Resources, December 2010. http://www.clir.org/pubs/reports/pub149/pub149.pdf

Kussman, Carol. (2012). "Checksum Verification Tools: Guest Post by Carol Kussmann." Practical E-Records blog. http://e-records.chrisprom.com/checksum-verification-tools/

Lee, Christopher A., et al. "Bitcurator: Tools and Techniques for Digital Forensics in Collecting Institutions." *D-Lib Magazine* 18 no. 5/6 (May/June 2012). http://www.dlib.org/dlib/may12/lee/05lee.html

Minnesota Historical Society. "Electronic Records Management Guidelines." http://www.mnhs.org/preserve/records/electronicrecords/erguidelinestoc.html

Mumma, Courtney, Glenn Dingwall, and Sue Bigelow. "A First Look at the Acquisition and Appraisal of the 2010 Olympic and Paralympic Winter Games Fonds: or, SELECT * FROM VANOC_Records AS Archives WHERE Value="true";" *Archivaria* 72 (Fall 2011): 92–122.

O'Meara, Erin, and Meg Tuomala. "Finding Balance Between Archival Principles and Real-Life Practices in an Institutional Repository." *Archivaria* 73 (Spring 2012): 81–103.

PARADIGM. *Workbook on Digital Private Papers*. http:/www.paradigm.ac.uk/workbook/index.html

Pearce-Moses, Richard. "An Arizona Model for Preservation and Access of Web Documents." *Dttp: Documents to the People* 33, no. 1 (Spring 2005): 17–24. http://www.azlibrary.gov/diggovt/documents/pdf/AzModel.pdf

Pearce-Moses, Richard. "Janus in Cyberspace: Archives on the Threshold of the Digital Era." *The American Archivist* 70 no. 1 (2007): 13–22.

Prom, Christopher. "Simple E-Records Preservation and Accesss Plan." Practical E-Records blog. http://e-records.chrisprom.com/recommendations/supported-formats/simple-e-records-preservation-and-access-plan/

———. "The Practical E-Records Method." Practical E-Records blog. http://e-records.chrisprom.com/recommendations/

———. "Making Digital Curation a Systematic Institutional Function." *The International Journal of Digital Curation* 1, no. 6 (2011): 139–52. http://www.ijdc.net/index.php/ijdc/article/view/169

Special Issue on Special Collections and Archives in the Digital Age. *Research Library Issues: A Quaerterly Report from ARL, CNI, and SPARC*, no. 279 (June 2012) http://publications.arl.org/rli279/

Society of American Archivists Campus Case Studies. (All). http://www2.archivists.org/publications/epubs/Campus-Case-Studies

Thomas, Susan, and Janette Martin. "Using the Papers of Contemporary British Politicians as a Testbed for the Preservation of Digital Personal Archives." *Journal of the Society of Archivists* 27, no.1 (2006): 29–56.

Thomas, Susan, Renhard Gittens, Janette Martin, and Fran Baker. "Paradigm: Workbook on Personal Digital Archives." Oxford: Bodleian Library, 2007. http://www.paradigm.ac.uk/workbook/index.html

Web Tools

ABC Amber Outlook Convertor (email conversion)
http://www.processtext.com/abcoutlk.html

Aid4Mail2 (email conversion)
http://www.aid4mail.com/

Archive-It Web Archiving Service
http://www.archive-it.org/

Archivematica
http://archivematica.org

BitCurator Tool
http://www.bitcurator.net/

California Digital Library's Web Archiving Service
http://webarchives.cdlib.org/

Catweasel
http://www.jschoenfeld.com/products/catweasel_e.htm

Chronopolis (digital preservation network)
http://chronopolis.sdsc.edu/

Curator's Workbench (Ingest and description tool)
http://www.lib.unc.edu/blogs/cdr/index.php/2010/12/01/announcing-the-curators-workbench/

DROID (Digital Record Object Identification)
http://sourceforge.net/projects/droid/

Duke DataAccessioner (Ingest tool)
    http://library.duke.edu/uarchives/about/tools/data-accessioner.html

FITS (File Information Tool Set)
    http://code.google.com/p/fits

Forensic Toolkit Imager
    http://accessdata.com/support/adownloads

Hosted Open Repository (DSpace-based commercial hosted solution)
    http://www.openrepository.com

HTTrack (local website copying app)
    http://www.httrack.com

Isilon (commercial storage platform)
    http://www.isilon.com

L.I.F.E. (Life Cycle Information for E-Literature
    http://www.life.ac.uk/

OnBase (commercial enterprise content management system)
    http://www.hyland.com/onbase-and-ecm.aspx

Practical E-Records software and tools for archivists
    http://e-records.chrisprom.com/resources/software/

QuickView Plus (view and appraise files without opening them)
    http://www.avantstar.com/metro/home/products/quickviewplusstandardedition

SobekCM
    http://ufdc.ufl.edu/sobekcm

YouSendIt (online file sharing software)
    https://www.yousendit.com/

Note: All URLs accessed July 18, 2012.

Made in the USA
Lexington, KY
10 September 2012